VEGAN MEXICO

Also by Jason Wyrick

Vegan Tacos

VEGAN MEXICO

Soul-Satisfying Regional Recipes from Tamales to Tostadas

Jason Wyrick

Vegan Heritage Press
Woodstock • Virginia

ISBN 13: 978-1-941252-21-5

First Edition, November 2016
10 9 8 7 6 5 4 3

Vegan Heritage Press, LLC books are available at quantity discounts. For information, please visit our website at www.veganheritagepress.com or write the publisher at Vegan Heritage Press, P.O. Box 628, Woodstock, VA 22664-0628.

Library of Congress Cataloging-in-Publication Data

> Names: Wyrick, Jason, author.
> Title: Vegan Mexico: soul-satisfying regional recipes from tamales to
>   tostadas / Jason Wyrick.
> Description: First edition. | Woodstock, Virginia: Vegan Heritage Press,
>   [2016] | Includes index. | Description based on print version record and
>   CIP data provided by publisher; resource not viewed.
> Identifiers: LCCN 2016022003 (print) | LCCN 2016019244 (ebook) | ISBN
>   9781941252222 (epub) | ISBN 9781941252239 (prc) | ISBN 9781941252215 (pbk.)
> Subjects: LCSH: Cooking, Mexican. | LCGFT: Cookbooks.
> Classification: LCC TX716.M4 (print) | LCC TX716.M4 W97 2016 (ebook) | DDC
>   641.5972--dc23

Photo credits: Front cover: stock photo. Interior photos by Jason Wyrick. Incidental stock photos. Cover design by Dianne Wenz.

Disclaimer: Allergies can be a serious threat to one's health. If you know you have food allergies, please take necessary precautions whenever you cook. Also, gloves and eye protection are recommended for handling hot chiles. If you require a medical diagnosis, or if you are contemplating any major dietary change, please consult a qualified health-care provider. You should always seek an expert medical opinion before making changes in your diet.

Vegan Heritage Press, LLC books are distributed by Andrews McMeel Publishing.

Printed in the United States of America

Dedication

This book is dedicated to the women in my family who passed down to me our family's traditional Mexican recipes, to my mom who passed to me our family's rich, and sometimes crazy history, and to my wife and daughter for their love and support and infinite willingness to taste test the recipes in this book.

Contents

VEGAN MEXICO

Trying to encapsulate the cuisine of a country as diverse as Mexico in one book, or even five books, is a fool's errand at best. However, I can give you a glimpse into the melting-pot world of Mexican food that will turn your kitchen into una cocina Mexicana.

In this book, I provide a mix of many popular Mexican recipes, from Chilaquiles to Red Pozole, and recipes that are rarely seen outside of their home regions, such as Pirate Tacos from Monterey. In many cases, these recipes are exactly like the traditional recipes. Other recipes are my vegan translations of dishes that are normally meat heavy, such as chilorio, a dish traditionally made with shredded pork in chile sauce.

Nearly all of the ingredients are easy to find, with substitutions given for those that aren't. My hope, however, is that authentic Mexican food inspires you enough to set out in search of these "mysterious" ingredients. In terms of skill, the recipes run the gamut from simple to complex, but most are right in the middle. If you have a little experience in the kitchen, you'll find these recipes quite doable.

Finally, I chose recipes that are designed to teach essential techniques for creating Mexican food, so that you can pick up any Mexican cookbook and make your own vegan versions of traditional nonvegan recipes. It will open up a vast world of Mexican food for you to call upon and explore!

My book *Vegan Tacos: Authentic and Inspired Recipes for Mexico's Favorite Street Food* (also published by Vegan Heritage Press) is an important companion to this book. *Vegan Tacos* is not just a book on tacos but on salsas, gear, tortilla-making, chiles, drinks like horchata and café de olla, and a whole lot more. Plus, it's one of the most extensive guides on tacos in the world. For space reasons, I have tried not to repeat too much of the information from *Vegan Tacos* in *Vegan Mexico*. If you like this book, and you like authentic tacos, I urge you to pick up a copy of *Vegan Tacos*. For now, however, I hope you enjoy exploring the delights of *Vegan Mexico*.

Mi Familia

To me, Mexican food means family. My Mexican ancestry comes from my mom's side. Our ancestors were primarily Spanish—specifically Basque—but the family has been a part of Mexico for well over a century, their identity woven into the Mexican cultural landscape, including food. Especially food. I remember visiting our relatives when I was very young and always being offered foods like beans, tacos, tamales, and huevos rancheros.

I should qualify my Mexican food exposure, however, lest this turn into "see how Mexican I am" street-cred bragging. The food I grew up with was what I call "Mexicanish." At the time, most of the Mexican food in the Phoenix area was heavily Americanized, laden with cheddar cheese and dull enchilada sauces. Tacos were made with flour tortillas or hard shells, not the fresh, soft corn tortillas of Mexico, and the same dishes repeated ad nauseam on restaurant menus. Missing were the vibrant, fresh foods that could be found just across the border: salads of fresh fruit dressed with lime and chile powder, rich moles, and soul-satisfying caldos (soups).There was one special exception. I could always get good tamales. Somehow, tamales made it across the border unscathed. At home, my parents both worked and had to take care of three boys, so we didn't get as many home-cooked meals as we liked, but when we did, they were amazing. My mom made the best enchiladas and tamales and Mexican red rice. I still crave those childhood foods, so when I became a vegan chef in my thirties, I decided to explore my family's food heritage. I am so glad I did.

Mexican food is about friends and family. It's about fresh ingredients and chiles. It's about sharing, throwing big parties, spontaneity. And it's about the eating. Mexicans, my mom's family included, are fixated on food. My mom told me a story about how, after the women in the family were done playing cards, her aunt Marta would ask if anyone was hungry (the answer was always yes!) and head into the kitchen to make chiles rellenos, simply because that's what they did. I learned about how my grandmother and great-grandmother made fresh tortillas every day for breakfast, to be eaten with butter and jam. She told me stories about how all the women would come to the house for two or three days to make tamales for holidays or elaborate parties, often two- to three-hundred people strong. The largest one was for over a thousand people, in honor of my mom's cousin after she was named Miss Mexico. I regularly cater for large groups, but I have a professional staff on board. They were doing that all by themselves and from the stories they tell, I think they would have put me to shame.

From my family, I learned about all the fresh flavors and fruits and vegetables in their kitchens and about how they made a salad to go with every meal. I laughed when I heard about how they put chiles in everything, because I've done the same without coaching. They reminisced about the earthy aroma of cooking beans and gossiped about all the gossip that happens when you get a bunch of friends and family together in one spot. (And I think I got the tame versions of those stories.) I also listened to tales about sharing and camaraderie in the kitchen. From my family's stories about food, I learned about family itself. Now I know why it drove my mom crazy when none of us boys wanted to sit down together at dinner time. Sorry, Mom.

Food should be shared and experienced together. There's nothing more Mexican than that, and so I share these recipes with you in the hope that they inspire you to make some of those same connections. Maybe someday you and I will share a meal together.

What Makes It Mexican?

The droll answer to this question is that it's made in Mexico, but in a way, there's truth to that. I've noticed when I talk with people about Mexican food, many of think about it as though it's this singular monolithic cuisine. I don't blame anyone for it. We like to categorize things into easy packets of digestible information, but Mexican cuisine doesn't like to play by the rules. How can it? Mexico is one of the largest countries

in the world, and was one of the largest empires during the 1800s. At one point, Mexico encompassed most of the Western half of the United States, from Texas up to Canada, and all of modern Mexico, which extends to the northern border of Guatemala. Its ecology is hugely diverse, ranging from hot northern deserts to cool tropical mountains. Its history is just as varied, with influences from the Olmecs, Mayans, Aztecs, pre-Columbian North Americans, post-Columbian North Americans, Spanish, French, Austrians, Middle Easterners, Japanese, and Chinese, just to name a few. That's why it's so hard to define Mexican cuisine and make claims on what is authentic and what isn't. It's why the easiest answer is simply to say that Mexican cuisine is food normally made in Mexico. But that's not entirely true either, because Mexican cuisine has certainly transcended the country's borders, and if you're holding this book in your hands—I'm assuming you're not in Mexico—then it has even made its way to you.

Perhaps there are no hard-and-fast rules, but there are a few common themes. The first, and most important, is that the food is lively! It pops with flavor, whether from spicy chiles, fresh citrus, or sweet fruit. It's complex. Why settle for a sauce made from one chile when you can make it from two? There's a preponderance of fresh produce. The climate and geography of Mexico make it one of the prime growing regions in the world, and Mexican cuisine capitalizes on that. There's a prolific use of chiles. They may not be in every dish, but they're in a lot of them—even in drinks and desserts. Then there's corn and masa. It's everywhere, even if it's just in a side of fresh tortillas. Finally, Mexican food is a social experience, whether that's going out with friends or cooking a big meal with family. The shared experience of making food, sharing it, and eating is a big part of the Mexican table. Chiles and corn, fresh produce, lively complex flavors, shared with friends and family. That's what makes Mexican food the jazzy progressive metal of the culinary world.

Each Mexican region has its own take on these overarching themes, influenced by several predominating factors. First and foremost is simply what's grown there, which is based on geography and climate. Southern Mexico has more tropical fruits than the northern desert city of Hermosilla, and both regional cuisines reflect that. Second is how close an area was to a place of Spanish power or a Spanish mission. For example, the port of Veracruz was the most important port in Spanish Mexico, so tons (literally!) of Spanish foods came through Veracruz. You can see that with the use of raisins, olive oil, and olives in the food of that region, whereas some of the mountainous areas in the Yucatán peninsula, an area that was notoriously hard for the Spanish to control, have a cuisine that looks more Mayan than Spanish. Trading partners have also helped influence the different cuisines of Mexico. The Gulf of Mexico side manifests an Afro-Caribbean influence that the Pacific side doesn't, while Baja is influenced by Southern California and even Japanese tourism. Finally, immigration has played a part in shaping regional cuisine and Mexico has certainly had its share of immigration, from Lebanese to Chinese to American expats.

Following is a very general rundown of the culinary regions of Mexico, and my apologies to those I left out and for the generalizations. I could write a couple cookbooks dedicated to each region.

The Regions

Oaxaca – Pronounced "wuh-HAH-cuh," this is one of the most famous culinary regions, known for its staggering amount of chiles, tiny avocados with a subtle anise-like flavor and edible skin called criollos, moles, black beans, coffee, chocolate, and mezcal. Oaxaca has mountains, valleys, and coastlines, allowing for a large diversity of ingredients, and Oaxacans use those to make complex, rich, fragrant dishes.

Veracruz – Veracruz is a major port city, and was the major port city of Spanish Mexico. The influences of Spanish and Afro-Cuban cooking are strong there. Want a Spanish empanada? You can get one in Vera-

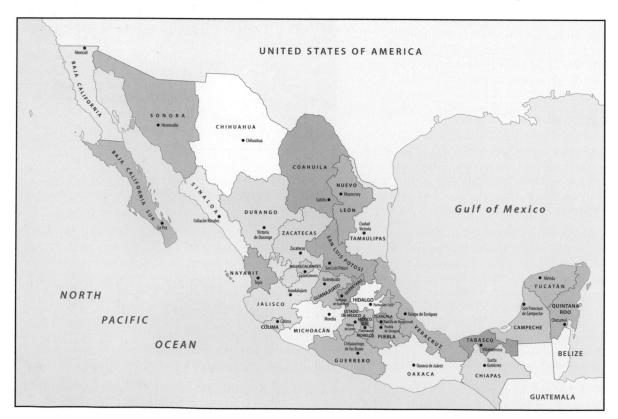

cruz. The cuisine is a heady mix of fresh fruits, beans, corn, saffron, chiles, tomatoes, olives, capers, olive oil, cumin, cilantro, bay leaves, and cinnamon. It's the epicenter of the introduction of citrus and olives to Mexico.

Yucatán – Yucatecan food reflects a strong Mayan influence, and you can still find precolonial recipes being made outside the big cities. In fact, many of these dishes still go by their Mayan names. Yucatecan cuisine is famous for its roasting pits, called pibils, to which super-heated stones are added and the pit covered with maguey (a type of agave) leaves that impart a unique flavor to the food. It's also known for earthy red achiote, also called annatto. The cuisine leans toward the spicy side and is known for mixing strong acidic flavors and heat, like the classic Yucatecan condiment of pickled onions and habanero chiles. It's also known for its spice mixes, called recados, and for its use of sour Seville oranges. There is also a strong Lebanese immigrant culture, which has given some of the regional recipes a Middle Eastern flair.

Distrito Federal – This region, colloquially named DF, contains Mexico City and its surroundings. This is where the cuisines of the different regions collide with international cuisines and show up both in high-end experimental restaurants and in the most vibrant street-food culture the world has to offer. DF has the most diverse food culture in Mexico, and because it has so many foreign visitors and expats, there are plenty of options that are a little friendlier to those who aren't used to the searing, intense flavors that are found in other parts of the country.

Northern Mexico – Northern Mexico is the wheat-growing breadbasket of Mexico and has been since Spanish colonial times. In the north, wheat plays almost as important a role as corn. In fact, there are over forty different types of wheat tortillas found in El Norte. It's huge, wide-open farmland that, ironically, doesn't see a lot of rainfall, so there is a wide use of dried ingredients. Unfortunately, it is also cattle country, so the north can be meat- and cheese-heavy. In this book, I use mushrooms, jackfruit, and the occasional piece of seitan to replicate these dishes. Many of the adaptations to Mexican food served in the United States are based on Northern Mexican dishes.

Northern Border Towns – Although the food from northern border towns is not traditionally considered a unique category when talking about Mexican cuisine, I've found in my travels that the food in border towns is more heavily influenced than the rest of Northern Mexico by places such as Tucson, San Diego, and El Paso. In return, these US cities are influenced by Heroica Nogales, Tijuana, and Ciudad Juarez. Burritos, chimichangas, burgers, and wheat flour tacos are common dishes found along the border.

Baja – Baja is known for its fresh dishes like ceviche, and being around seafood in Baja is inescapable. I use hearts of palm and trumpet and oyster mushrooms to achieve many of the same flavors and textures. In the touristy areas, the food of Baja is designed to cater to Americans and Japanese. Soy sauce can be found at taco bars in the region and tempura-battered ingredients are a common sight. Baja also has a strong Spanish influence as it was one of the prime areas where Catholic missions were established. You can find traditional paella still served in Baja. Baja is also Mexico's largest wine-producing region, and recipes containing wine are readily found. It's a mix of mainland Mexican and California-type food with a little Asian thrown in for good measure.

Puebla and Central Mexico – Poblano cuisine is known for mole, pipián (sauces made from seeds), adobo, dark dried chiles, poblano chiles, and a thousand different ways to use pepitas (hulled squash seeds). Spanish and French influences are strong here and panaderías (Mexican bakeries) look almost like French patisseries. Poblano cuisine is sauce-heavy, and the sauces are often thickened with various nuts and seeds. Like DF, this region is a nexus for world cuisine, but I feel like the Mexican filter is a little stronger in Puebla.

Western Mexico – This includes the regions of Michoacán, Jalisco, and Colima. These foods tend to be spicy and sweet, with plenty of chile-based stews and soups and rice dishes. Some of my favorite caldos come from these regions. These areas have less of a Spanish influence than eastern and central Mexico and use corn more heavily. Here, you can find dishes made from corn masa, mixed with fresh corn, and steamed in corn reeds served alongside corn-based soups and a stack of corn tortillas. This area is known for its diversity of tamales, which come in a dizzying variety of shapes, fillings, and wrappers.

Southern Mexico – Southern Mexico is heavy on tropical fruits, and it's easier to find dishes that are less spicy than other areas of Mexico. There are certainly searing-hot dishes, but in places like Chiapas, sweet is preferred over heat. The region is known for sweet drinks, and many of the dishes have a rustic quality to them. The South has interesting sweet, tropical twists on classic dishes, like horchata made with coconut milk instead of dairy milk, and chiles rellenos commonly stuffed with fruit.

The History of Mexico on One Plate

The cuisine of Mexico is rich and complex, like its history. The land has been ruled by at least five different empires, sometimes in rapid succession. Mexican food incorporates thousands of years of Mesoamerican cooking with Spanish and Middle Eastern culture, as well as influences from as far away as Southeast Asia and India. It's a mélange of ingredients and techniques, always filtered through a Mexican lens, that come together to create one of the most exquisite cuisines of the world. Like language, food reflects the history of cultures colliding, and we can trace that history in this one plate of food: bean and squash blossom tamales in mole Poblano.

Let's start with the tamale itself, the perfect combination of ancient agriculture and food practices from at least as far back as 1500 BCE. The three primary ingredients in this tamale—beans, squash, and corn—comprised the basic nutrition building blocks of all Mesoamerican societies. Beans, which apparently had two periods of domestication, appear to have first been domesticated in the Lerma-Santiago Basin in west central Mexico. They have been found near sites that nomadic tribes used for support, providing a supply of dry, edible food as proof against starvation. Once domestication of this vital protein occurred, more permanent settlements could arise. Beans were so effective in providing the protein basis for society, they are still the primary protein source in Mexico today. Plus, they're tasty. That's why they're in our tamale!

Corn (or maize, if you will), arguably the most important crop in the history of Mexico, was originally a grass called teosinte that scarcely resembles the plant we see today. However, the seeds of the teosinte plant could be popped over intense heat and, like beans, was nutrient-dense. In one of the slowest genetic modifications of a plant for human consumption, a project begun about nine thousand years ago, teosinte was bred to have bigger and softer, more consumable kernels, eventually developing into the huge ears of corn we see today. This crop didn't achieve major importance, however, until it was discovered 3,500 years ago in Guatemala that soaking the dry kernels in a highly alkaline solution (water and ash) allowed the kernels to be ground into sticky dough (which, unknown to them, was due to the release of niacin).

Corn, when processed this way and combined with beans, provides every amino acid the human body needs, creating the vaunted complete protein. Cue the monolith music from *2001: A Space Odyssey*, because that's how important this domestication was to Mesoamerican cultures. And like beans, corn also happens to be very tasty. This newly discovered corn dough was turned into thick tortillas, cakes, dumplings, and yes, tamales, which evidence shows have been eaten for at least twenty-five hundred years.

> ### The Three Sisters
>
> The Three Sisters (beans, squash, and corn), are a dynamic culinary trio of plants used throughout the western world. Mesoamerican society, until the Spanish conquest, was almost entirely plant-based. But it was the Spanish penchant for animal products that moved the culinary focus in that direction.

Corn and beans dominate our tamale, but it still has one more important ingredient, and that's the squash blossom. Squash, beans, and corn are the foundation crops, not just for Mesoamerica but for North and South America, as well. Half the planet was fed on this trio of plants known as the Three Sisters. Out of the three, squash was the earliest plant to be cultivated, starting around 8000 BCE. Not only did squash provide sustenance and nutrition but it also could be preserved and its shells used as tools. When the three plants were combined, the bean runners used the corn stalks as support, and the squash plants provided ground cover that prevented weeds, animals, and insects from inhabiting the garden. So, our tamale is built upon the foundation of Mesoamerican society itself.

Enter mole poblano, our world-fusion sauce featuring three different chiles, chocolate, a host of spices, sugar, bread, tortillas, onions, plantains, garlic, nuts, and seeds, all ground into a rich paste that is fried and simmered to perfection. We've covered where the tortillas and pepitas found in the recipe originate, but where do all those other ingredients come from? Like the corn, beans, and squash, chiles are Mesoamerican in origin, originally cultivated around Puebla. (No wonder they show up in mole poblano!) However, it was the commercial reach of the Aztec empire that brought so many diverse chiles into one area, allowing for complex chile sauces to be made. The reach of the empire extended from the south of Mexico all the way into what is now modern Arizona, and the empire's trade routes extended well beyond that. Utilizing the road system of the Aztec empire, which rivaled that of Rome, trade goods could move from Peru to the south of North America and from there spread out to places as far away as Mississippi.

Tomatoes and tomatillos were native plants in the Puebla region, used in much the same way as they're used now, so they are an obvious addition to our sauce. Chocolate, another essential ingredient in mole poblano, was brought out of the conquered Mayan territories in and around Yucatán by the Aztecs. However,

chocolate was sacred and normally reserved for royalty, so while it made its way to the region, it wasn't quite ready for our mole.

We're almost there! We can see our mole poblano start to form, thanks to the reach and organization of Aztec rule, which brought diverse ingredients together to a central region. What are we still missing? Aromatic spices, bread, onions, garlic, raisins, sugar, almonds, sesame seeds, and oil.

Those ingredients weren't known until the Spanish conquest of the early 1500s, but the history of those ingredients actually begins in Asia. The spice routes of the ancient world brought oranges, limes, pepper, sesame seeds, coriander (cilantro) seeds, cinnamon, anise, and cumin from India, China, and Southeast Asia to the Middle East, whose people added onions and garlic and sent them to Rome in modest quantities. The Crusades further introduced these spices to Europe. However, it was the Muslim conquest of the Iberian Peninsula, beginning in 711 CE and lasting until 1492 CE, that made these ingredients integral to Spanish cuisine. Spain may have kicked the Moors out at the battle of Granada, but the Spanish must have thought the food was delicious, because they retained all the spices, citrus trees, and culinary trends, which were then brought in force—literally—to the New World just a few decades later. It's hard to imagine Mexican cuisine without cumin, cilantro, citrus, onions, and garlic, but before the Spanish, those ingredients were nonexistent in Mexico.

Puebla and Poblanos

"Poblano" simply means "from Puebla de Los Angeles," so mole Poblano means a mole from Puebla and a Poblano is a person from Puebla.

The Spanish also brought raisins and almonds from Europe and sugar from the Caribbean to add to our mole, and they brought their frying techniques with them, too, which did not exist in Mesoamerica until then. Yes, you can blame (or celebrate, if you prefer) all the fried Mexican foods on the Spanish.

You may be wondering who created this crazy concoction with such a massive ingredient list that takes a few hours to properly put together. The answer is the nuns that lived at the Convent of Santa Rosa in the sixteenth century. Supposedly, the archbishop of the area announced a surprise visit to the convent. The nuns went into a panic to make something special for him, so they began putting together this impromptu sauce to impress him. Ingredients kept being added, like raisins, almonds, and chocolate. The sauce kept slowly cooking, condensing in flavor. Evidently, the archbishop was impressed and the sauce became legendary, because mole poblano is the most famous dish of modern-day Puebla.

Ironically, the idea of using chocolate to flavor a dish like this was abhorrent to the Aztecs, because it was sacred to them. So, the particular combination of ingredients to make mole poblano required a Catholic hand. It constantly amazes me the way different threads in history weave together to create our meals. Without the Catholic Church's desire to spread Christianity throughout Mexico, the Convent at Santa Rosa would not have been established, and mole poblano would most likely not exist!

There is one more ingredient in that mole that we haven't covered, and that's the bread. While the Spanish introduced wheat and, consequently, bread to Mexico, it was the replacement of rustic native bread by French bread, also known as "pan Frances," to mole poblano that gives us its modern incarnation. During the 1700s and into the early 1800s, quite a few French nationals moved to Mexico, and, not willing to live without their fine breads, started French bakeries.

While these French breads flourished and remained a part of Mexico, the French themselves did not. After Mexico gained its independence from Spain in 1821, the country was in turmoil. During the nineteenth century, civil war and invasions were more common than peacetime in Mexico. France had its own designs on the country and invaded Mexico twice. The second invasion resulted in France taking over the country and installing an Austrian emperor on the throne, Ferdinand Maximilian Joseph. His rule lasted only three years before the French abandoned him and the Mexican army retook their country. During that time, the emperor imported some of the finest chefs from Europe, who, at the time, specialized in French cuisine. That's why you see dishes like crêpes and cream-based dishes in Mexican food. It was also the height of French bakeries in the big cities. Once the French left Mexico, and their puppet emperor was executed, many French nationals left, and, like when the Moors left Spain, the people may have gone, but the food stayed.

And so the story of mole poblano is the story of most of the major culinary traditions from around the globe. There's a good reason why, when you go to Mexico, people say that you can eat the world. I have long thought that the story of food is a tale of geography, necessity, trade, and war. If you want to make the tamale with mole poblano, take the Pot of Beans recipe from page 29, add 4 chopped squash blossoms to the filling, dress the finished tamales with the Mole Poblano recipe from page 176, garnish with chopped cilantro, and serve with lime wedges and a cold beer. Now you've got a taste of world history wrapped up inside a simple tamale.

Molcajetes and majaderos

GEAR, INGREDIENTS, AND TECHNIQUES

Authentic Mexican food and the Mexican cocina have been rapidly gaining in popularity around the world over the last twenty years, but they can still be intimidating if you're unfamiliar with tortilla presses, cazuelas, cactus paddles, various chiles, and such.

F ear not, because getting your own cocina together is easy and fun, and you don't need much in the way of kitchen gear. I think you'll find that the new ingredients are an opportunity to explore new foods, but if you don't have access to them, you'll still get a lot out of *Vegan Mexico*. Most of those ingredients have substitutions, or can be omitted entirely, though I hope you'll opt to seek them out. You'll be amazed at the new flavors you'll discover!

Gear

Here are a few pieces of equipment that will help, the most important of which is a tortilla press. Technically, you can press tortillas with a heavy pan or other such object, but the tortilla press will make your life easier, and fresh tortillas are transformational. The second most important item is an iron skillet, which you can use for pan-roasting, a technique that I cover on page 18. It's also handy for cooking tortillas, frying, and baking. Those are the two essentials. You may also want a cazuela for cooking beans and making stews. It looks cool and lends a subtle flavor to dishes, but if you don't invest in one, you can easily use a pot to similar effect. Everything else is a specialized piece of equipment that's fun to have, but far from necessary.

Tortilla press – Tortillas used to be patted out by hand, and in some places in Mexico, they still are. I remember going to a tortilleria in Nogales and seeing the woman behind the counter patting out a tortilla in just a few seconds. Most people, however, use a tortilla press and the most common tortilla press is a hinged aluminum one. They are inexpensive, typically around $15, and make tortilla pressing a cinch. You can get them online, and a lot of grocery stores carry them. Even my local Target has tortilla presses. There are also cast iron tortilla presses, which will help make a super thin tortilla, but they require some practice and are about twice as expensive. If you really get into tortilla presses, you can find some old mesquite presses. They're heavy and also make very thin tortillas. They are as much works of art as they are utilitarian, and you should plan on spending at least $70 for one.

Iron skillet and griddle – Iron skillets are one of the most versatile tools in my kitchen. When I want to fry chiles, I add a layer of oil to the skillet. When I want to pan-roast chiles, onions, garlic, tomatillos, and the like, I crank up my iron skillet. I can bake giant chilaquiles in my skillet, make cakes, and, of course, sauté ingredients. My preferred one is 12 inches in diameter and has a 2 1/2-inch lip. You can also make tortillas in these, though I prefer an iron griddle as opposed to a skillet, because there's no lip to get in the way of my spatula. (I have an extra-large skillet that can cook about twelve tortillas at a time.) I like the iron, because it roughly mimics the flat clay cooking surface of a comale, traditionally used to make tortillas and roast ingredients.

Cazuelas – "Cazuela" is a catch-all name for an earthenware stew pot. Some are wide and shallow while others resemble lidded pots. They come in sizes anywhere from just a few inches in diameter, ideal for making a single serving of something, to large 20-inch versions for making giant batches of guisados (thick stews). I use my lidded cazuelas for making beans and my large cazuela for guisados. Many cazuelas are decorated, and you can transfer them directly from the stove or oven to the table. My Mexican market sells a few different cazuelas and you can order them online. Be aware that many cazuelas are still lead-glazed, but that's changing. I always investigate when purchasing a new cazuela. I ordered my large one online from La Tienda and my small pot-like ones from a Mexican pottery shop, both lead-free.

Molcajete and tejolote – These are basically a mortar and pestle made out of rough basalt, though I've seen a number of them made out of pebbled concrete. These are perfect for making guacamole, crushed salsa, chile pastes, garlic pastes, and anything else you need to smash. They are very heavy, so be careful when you lift them. You can get by with a regular mortar and pestle, but nothing quite creates the same texture as a good molcajete (the base) and tejolote (the crusher). You can find these at a Mexican market, specialty store, or online, and I've even seen them at Macy's. They're not too expensive and they make a nice centerpiece. Because they're made of stone, you can even roast in them and serve directly to the table!

Huarache and sope presses – Similar to a tortilla press, these are designed specifically to press out sandal-shaped huaraches and thick, round sopes, both of which are types of masa cakes. You can make huaraches and sopes by hand without much problem, so I don't consider these necessary, only helpful when making those specific dishes.

Clockwise from top left: metal comal, tortilla press (tortilladora), tortillas in a taco warmer, a molcajete and tejolote, molino, (center) a clay comal, and a cazuela.

1. Jalapeño
2. Poblano
3. Habanero
4. Serrano
5. Chilaca
6. Fresh Chiles de Árbol
7. Guero
8. Pequín
9. Dried Chiles de Árbol
10. Negro/Pasilla (dried chilaca)
11. Guajillo
12. Ancho
13. Chipotle Morita
14. Cascabel
15. Chipotle Meco

Ingredients

Mexico is a produce-heavy country, and a lot of the flavor in authentic Mexican cuisine comes through the use of high-quality fresh fruits and vegetables. You may be surprised to learn that the Mexican markets in the United States often have better quality produce than what you can find at a regular grocery store. Because these markets cater to the Mexican community, they are great places to get chiles, cactus paddles, herbs (such as epazote and hoja santa), and lot of other ingredients you don't usually see. I urge you to find a Mexican market in your local area and check it out. I think you'll be surprised.

Following is a list of ingredients that are used in this book, but may not be staples in your kitchen. Some of them are optional ingredients for a few of the recipes, while others, like ancho and guajillo chiles, are frequently used ingredients. **Please Note:** Ingredients that are essential for making the recipes in this book are shown in **orange**.

Dried Chiles

Guajillo chiles – These long, dried red chiles are the dried version of the mirasol chile. They have a leathery skin and a toasted caramel undertone. They're one of the essential chiles for making chile-based sauces and they can also be used to make chile powders. Ideally, they should be toasted or fried before being rehydrated for use in a sauce.

Ancho chiles – These red chiles are so dark that they appear nearly black and are the other type of chile used to make most chile-based sauces. They are frequently used in conjunction with guajillos to create a complex chile flavor. They have fruity, caramel undertones and are wide at the top ("ancho" means wide) with a wrinkly blackish skin. An ancho chile is the dried version of the poblano chile, and it is often used interchangeably with pasilla chiles.

Chiles de árbol – These small, hot chiles are used to spike soups and stews with heat or are ground up to make spicy salsas. While you can find fresh versions of these, they are most commonly found and used dried. Their flavor is best when toasted, but they should only be toasted for a few seconds.

Chipotles – Chipotles are smoked, dried jalapeños. There are two types of chipotles based on two strains of jalapeños. Chipotles mecos look like dried, tan tobacco leaves and are the most common type of chipotle. They're the ones used to make chipotles in adobo and they have a heavy, smoky, spicy taste. Chipotles morita are very dark colored chipotles that have a slightly sweeter taste than chipotles mecos. These are most often used to make salsas.

Pasilla chiles and chiles negros – These are long, thin black chiles used to make some moles and sauces. They have a flavor similar to an ancho chile but are not quite as fruity. In this book, they are primarily used in mole Poblano.

Mulato Chiles – Mulato chiles are similar to ancho chiles, both in appearance and in volume, and that's no coincidence. Mulato chiles are a dried version of a particular type of poblano chile (the fresh chile that turns into an ancho chile) that is left to mature on the vine until they achieve a very dark hue. They are spicier than ancho chiles and have a fruitier flavor with smokey notes of tobacco. They are part of the trinity of chiles that comprise dark moles like mole Poblano.

Fresh Chiles

Poblano chiles – These are the standard chile used to make many green chile sauces and rajas, which are strips of roasted green chile. Poblanos can be roasted and puréed, sliced and used fresh, or chopped and put into stews. They have a forest-green color and are fairly large. You can find them at most grocery stores. Make sure the skin looks tight and vibrant; otherwise, the poblano is on its way out. I sometimes use Hatch chiles as a substitute for poblanos when Hatch chile season rolls around here in the Southwest.

Serrano chiles – These are medium-size, thin green chiles known for their heat. Most of these chiles are just a couple inches in length, but some can get up to 5 inches in length. For the best chile, look for a tight skin. Sometimes these have an orange color to them, indicating ripeness, which means that they are both hotter and sweeter than normal.

Jalapeños – Small green chiles of medium heat, these are used to form the "hot" base for salsa. The pickled versions are a common condiment for tacos, tortas, and other antojitos. There are also red jalapeños, which are the ripe version of what is normally seen in grocery markets. The ripe ones are a little hotter and a little sweeter than their green counterparts.

Habaneros – Little bulbous firecrackers, these are used for both flavor and intense heat. Rarely used fresh, they are more often used as part of a pickling solution, to add heat to a sauce, or served pickled as a condiment for those who love heat. When used to flavor a soup or stew, the seeds are usually removed. They are most commonly orange, but you can find yellow and red ones as well.

Banana chiles, chiles gueros, and yellow wax chiles – These are different names for the same basic chile. They're medium-size yellow chiles that are a bit on the hot side but not overly so. They're pan-roasted for sauces and chopped or left whole to flavor soups.

Herbs and Spices

Mexican oregano – Called Mexican oregano because it looks like Greek and Italian oregano, it is used in much the same way. Mexican oregano is actually a type of verbena. It has a bright, lemony quality to it. You can use it fresh or dried, and if it's not available where you live, you can substitute an equal amount of marjoram.

Epazote – This leaf herb has a unique flavor for which there's no good substitute. The long, jagged leaves are best used fresh. It's used to flavor bean dishes (where it supposedly aids with indigestion) and is a popular addition to quesadillas, tacos, and soups. The leaves will droop and look wilted very quickly, but the epazote is still good. I usually have to get fresh epazote at my local Mexican market. If you can't get a hold of it, simply omit it from the recipe.

Hoja santa – A large, heart-shaped leaf with a very unique, poppy herbal flavor. Like epazote, there is no real substitute for hoja santa, but if you don't have it, it's easy to simply omit from the recipe. It's used in mole amarillo, to make certain teas, and as a wrapper for some tamales. It also goes by the names yerba santa and sacred leaf.

Canela, Mexican cinnamon, and Ceylon cinnamon – Canela has a robust, powerful flavor and is soft enough that it can be ground up in a molcajete. Its flavor really bursts when it's roasted for a couple minutes. If you don't have canela, simply substitute a common cinnamon stick.

Achiote paste and recado rojo – This Yucatecan spice mix is made from ground annatto, cinnamon, cloves, allspice, pepper, cumin, garlic, and, ideally, the juice of sour oranges. Its popularity extends well outside Yucatán, and it is used to roast veggies, as an addition to sauces, and as a rub for recipes like tacos al pastor. You can find achiote at nearly every Mexican market and it is easy to obtain online. There is no substitute for it.

Veggies and Fruits

Nopales/cactus paddles – These are prickly pear paddles and, while they are not widely used in the United States, they are a common vegetable in Mexico. The whole paddle is called a nopal and the slices are called nopalitos. When purchasing a cactus paddle, look for a fresh, vibrant color to the paddle with no wrinkling on the skin. Many markets sell them already trimmed. You can also by freshly cut no-palitos. If you need to trim the needles from the cactus, hold the paddle with tongs and scrape the needles away with the back of your knife. Then use the tip of your knife to remove the little nodules that contained the needles. Cut the rim of the paddle away and it's ready for slicing, grilling, or however you wish to use it. Once heated, nopales are slimy like okra, but the slime will cook away.

> ### Shopping Tip
> Food is an exhilarating adventure to me, so I write about finding and exploring new ingredients like I'm on a grand quest. Perhaps it's not like that for you and you simply want to get in, get out, and get to cooking. Your quest will be brief and successful if you head to your local Mexican market, which should have ingredients like epazote, all the chiles you need, piloncillo, and more.

Huitlacoche – Huitlacoche is a fungus that grows on corn and is harvested as a delicacy. It has a very earthy taste and isn't that easy to find fresh outside of Mexico. It's typically sold canned or jarred in the United States. The flavor is strong, so a little bit goes a long way. It can be found as a quesadilla or taco filling or as a filling for Mexican crêpes.

Pozole/hominy – Pozole is nixtamalized corn and is a great addition to soups and stews. It is the ingredient after which the soup, pozole, is named. Most Mexican markets sell fresh pozole every day, but you can get cans of pozole at many supermarkets.

Sour oranges/Seville oranges – These oranges are used to make sour orange juice, a popular flavoring agent for sauces and marinades. Sour oranges aren't always that easy to find, but you can easily substitute the juice of one naval orange mixed with the juice of one lime. I know other people add about 1/4 cup of grapefruit juice to that, but I can't stand grapefruit juice, so I never use it.

Avocados – All of the recipes in this book assume you are using Hass avocados.

Tomatoes – The tomatoes used throughout this book are Roma tomatoes, which are also called plum tomatoes.

Tomatillos – Always husk tomatillos before using, unless you are pan-roasting them.

Other Ingredients

Chipotles in adobo – These are chipotles marinated in a sauce made of ancho chiles, a little sugar, vinegar, and aromatic spices like cinnamon and allspice. That sauce is the adobo. Chipotles in adobo are commonly sold canned at most markets.

Masa and masa harina – Masa is the name for corn dough made from nixtamalized corn and ready to be turned into tortillas, tamales, sopes, and all the other corn dough–based dishes. You can make your own or purchase it fresh, and most Mexican markets will have bags of fresh masa out every morning. Masa harina is dried nixtamalized corn flour and is widely available. You can use masa harina to make your own masa and to thicken soups, stews, sauces, and even drinks, such as atole.

Piloncillo – This is a dark brown, unrefined sugar with a rich, deep taste. It's shaped like a pilon, hence the name, and can come in sizes ranging from one-ounce to one-pound pieces. It can be added as is when melting it, crushed in a molcajete, or grated. If you don't have piloncillo, you can substitute an equal amount of turbinado or brown sugar.

Pepitas – These are hulled, green pumpkin seeds that are used as condiments and as thickeners for sauces. When used raw, they have a very creamy quality. When toasted, they have a deep, nutty flavor. You can find these at places like Trader Joe's and your local Mexican market.

Pan-Roasting: The Most Important Technique in This Book

Pan-roasting is an easy way to re-create the charred flavor and texture of an open-flame grill without having to actually light your grill. It creates a flavor profile between sautéing and open-flame roasting. I much prefer this to oven-roasting because the flavor it creates is more intense and complex, and I live in Arizona. When it's 120°F in July, I do not want to turn on my oven or head outside and stand over an open fire. To pan-roast, take a heavy-bottomed pan, like an iron skillet, and bring it to medium heat. Place the ingredient directly on the hot, dry surface and wait (impatiently, if you're like me). Once the ingredient blisters, flip it and repeat until most sides are slightly blackened. You can pan-roast chiles, garlic, onions, tomatoes, tomatillos, squash, carrots, and other similar ingredients. If you are roasting garlic, leave the paper on the garlic as it protects the garlic cloves from burning.

CORN, BEANS, RICE, AND CHILES

Corn, beans, rice, and chiles are the heart of Mexican cuisine. They form the basic starch, protein, and seasonings for most meals. It's hard to imagine a Mexican meal without at least one of these staples at the table.

on't let the simplicity fool you, fresh corn tortillas are magical—or some Grilled Sweet Potatoes and Fennel (page 185). Rice typically shows up as a side dish, especially in Northern Mexico, and a pot of boiling beans can be found in nearly every cocina.

Set off on your Mexican food adventure by learning how to make these staple foods first. They are core components for many other Mexican dishes, like tortillas for tacos, or pintos borrachos for sopes, but they also make great meals all by themselves. I appreciate a good plate of rice and beans as much as a fancy five-star dinner—maybe even more so. It's simple and rustic, soulful and comforting, and exactly what I crave after a long day of work.

Corn, Masa, Tortillas, and More

It's impossible to talk about Mexican food without talking about corn and tortillas! Head to the streets of Mexico and you'll discover that most of the food stalls will be selling dishes featuring corn, like tacos, enchiladas, huaraches, gorditas, sopes, or even just grilled corn. Dine in a restaurant and chances are most of the items on the menu utilize corn in one fashion or another. Visit someone's home kitchen and expect to be greeted by a plate of warm corn tortillas. Read a book about Mexican food, and you're going to read about corn. To crib from Michael Pollan, we humans are corn's vector for worldwide dominance, and Mexican food is its agent provocateur (that last part is mine).

However, it's not just any type of corn that encapsulates the essence of Mexican cuisine. What really lies at the heart of most of these corn dishes is masa, which is a corn dough made from kernels that have been soaked with lime water or some other alkalinizing solution. It's masa that allows us to create tortillas, tamales, enchiladas, and most of the other street food served in Mexico. Below, you'll find recipes on how to make quick grilled corn, your own masa, and your own tortillas. Just as corn is the foundation for Mexican food, this section is the foundation for getting the most out of the recipes in this book.

Simple Grilled Corn
Elotes Asados

MAKES 4 SERVINGS

Grilled corn on its own is magnificent. Grilled corn laced with lime juice, chile powder, and salt makes me run outside to the grill and eat as many grilled corn cobs as I can get my hands on.

> **4 fresh ears corn**
> **Corn oil or melted vegan butter, optional**
> **Juice of 2 limes**
> **1 tablespoon chile powder (I prefer guajillo powder)**
> **1/2 teaspoon salt**

Light a grill. If using a gas grill, bring it to medium-high heat. Pull the corn husks back, but don't remove them from the corn. Remove as much of the silk as possible. Brush the oil onto the corn, if using. Grill the corn until it is browned but not blackened all around. Remove the corn from the grill and sprinkle it with lime juice, chile powder, and salt. Serve hot.

Making Masa

Masa is the name of the corn dough from which tortillas, gorditas, tamales, and similar items are made. It's made from nixtamalized corn, meaning the corn has been treated with an alkaline solution to loosen the pericarp of the individual kernels, make the niacin in them bio-available, and alter the starch in the corn in such a way as to allow it to stick together. Without nixtamalization, making corn tortillas would be impossible, and without corn tortillas, tacos wouldn't exist.

You can make homemade masa by cooking your own nixtamal and grinding it with a corn grinder, but it is a lot of work, something reserved for only the most die-hard food crafters. Fortunately, you can also make fresh masa by taking masa harina and mixing it with hot water. Masa harina is just dried ground nixtamalized corn and chances are your local grocery market carries masa harina.

The most common brand is Maseca, and Bob's Red Mill produces a non-GMO masa harina. I usually make my own masa when making tortillas and always when I am making tamales, huaraches, gorditas, and other similar dishes. The masa only takes a few minutes to make and the difference in flavor between tortillas made with fresh masa and store-bought is worth the effort.

Homemade Masa

MAKES 3 CUPS

2 cups masa harina
3/4 teaspoon salt
1 1/4 cups warm water

In a medium mixing bowl, combine the masa harina, salt, and water, working them by hand until they are incorporated together into a dough. Form the dough into a ball. The dough should be soft, but not stick to your hands. It should not be crumbly, either. Adjust the amount of masa harina or water as needed.

Let the dough rest for 10 minutes before using it, so that the masa harina can fully absorb the water. Cover the dough while it sits to keep the outer part from drying out.

From Masa to Tortillas

A Forgiving Art

Tortilla-making is an art, but it's a fairly forgiving art. Don't worry if your tortilla doesn't puff up. You'll still end up with a nice tortilla. If you want them a little extra toasty, you can increase the time you cook them. They won't be quite as pliable, but they will develop a more robust flavor.

Step 1: Place the testale and cover with plastic.

Step 2: Press the testale and peel off the plastic.

Step 3: Place on the griddle or comal to cook.

Step 4: Flip to cook on both sides.

Step 5: A finished tortilla ready to enjoy.

Making Corn Tortillas

There's nothing like a fresh corn tortilla. It's soulful, delicious, and perfect for scooping up beans, making tacos, or simply eating fresh off the griddle. You'll want an aluminum or small cast iron tortilla press (opposite) to make these. Don't worry, they're fairly inexpensive and will last a very long time. Unless you want an antique mesquite wood tortilla press, in which case they'll still last a very long time, but they are far from inexpensive!

Making corn tortillas is an art. It takes a little practice, but you'll be a master tortilladora once you get a feel for how much pressure to apply to the masa,

how hot the griddle should be, and how long the tortillas should stay on it (each batch is slightly different). The first one or two tortillas may not come out perfect, but that's part of the art. Don't worry if you don't get it right on the first try.

Traditionally, tortillas are made on a clay comal, which gives the tortillas a slight earthiness and helps toast them, but you can easily make them on a cast iron griddle, and I'm assuming that's how you'll do it. The cast iron acts much the same way as a comal and, unlike clay comales, cast iron griddles are easy to find. You can also make them in a heavy-bottomed pan, but they're a little more finicky than griddles and comales. You'll want a tortilla press when you make these. You can use a heavy skillet or glass baking dish to flatten them down, but tortilla presses are fairly inexpensive and making tortillas with them is very easy.

Basic Corn Tortillas

MAKES 10 (5-INCH) TORTILLAS

These tortillas are companions to many Mexican meals and even serve as the base for some. Whether you're making enchiladas, or just serving them with a wholesome pot of frijoles de olla, fresh, hand-made tortillas will take your meal from excellent to transformative.

1 1/4 cups masa

Heat a griddle to medium heat. Line both sides of a tortilla press with plastic wrap. Take enough corn dough to form a 1 1/2-inch ball and place the ball on the bottom plate of the tortilla press, just off-center and slightly toward the back hinge. Press the dough down firmly. Gently lift the top plate of the tortilla press. Remove the bottom piece of plastic wrap with the tortilla stuck to it and flip it upside down, so that the tortilla is against your palm. Peel away the plastic wrap, leaving just the tortilla in your hand.

Gently lay the tortilla on the griddle. If you slap it down, there's a good chance the tortilla will bubble. Once the edge of the tortilla looks a bit dry and starts to curl, about 45 seconds, flip the tortilla. (Use a spatula at first and as you practice, you may find you simply start using your fingers.) Cook the tortilla 1 minute. Flip it over again and cook another 15 seconds. Transfer the cooked tortilla to a basket, tortilla warmer, or plate, and cover with a towel to keep it warm and pliable. Repeat this process until you have used all your masa.

Basic Flour Tortillas

MAKES 8 TORTILLAS

Contrary to what some Mexican food aficionados would have you believe, flour tortillas do exist in Mexico, though they are primarily found in the north of Mexico and the melting pot of Mexican cuisine known as Mexico City. They're used for burritos, chivichangas (known here as chimichangas), or eaten simply as a snack.

> **1 1/2 cups unbleached all-purpose flour**
> **1/2 teaspoon salt**
> **1/2 teaspoon baking powder**
> **1/2 cup warm water**
> **1 tablespoon vegan shortening**

Combine the flour, salt, and baking powder in a mixing bowl. Add the water and shortening (skip this ingredient if you want a no-oil version) and combine until fully incorporated. Lightly flour a flat surface and knead the dough until it is elastic. Alternatively, you can use a stand mixer. Mix it at medium speed for 1 minute, then turn it down to low, mixing the dough until it is smooth.

Once your dough is ready, divide it into 8 balls, then flatten the balls in your palm. Set them down, cover with a towel, and let them rest for 15 minutes.

Heat a medium-size griddle or pan over medium-high heat. While the griddle is warming, lightly flour a work surface and roll each piece of dough into a 6- to 7-inch circle. After you finish rolling the first one, place it on the griddle and cook for 1 minute. Flip and cook for 30 seconds. Transfer the cooked tortilla to a plate or basket and cover with a towel. Repeat this process until you have cooked all the tortillas, keeping them covered so they stay pliable and warm.

Extra-Thick Tortillas for Gorditas, Saucy Tacos, and More

This recipe makes tortillas of moderate thickness. You can make your tortillas a bit thicker by not pressing as hard on the tortilla press. These extra-thick tortillas are great for making gorditas or for when you are serving them with particularly saucy toppings.

Chile-Flavored Tortillas

You can make chile-flavored tortillas by rehydrating 2 guajillo chiles (stemmed and seeded), puréeing the chiles in a blender or food processor until you have a smooth paste, and adding the purée to the dough when you first incorporate all the ingredients. You can also add fresh or roasted garlic for extra flavor. If you add the chile purée to your tortillas, remove 2 tablespoons of water from the above recipe.

Tostadas and Corn Chips

It's easy to make your own tostadas and corn chips. It's just a matter of drying out some tortillas and frying them in oil. If you don't dry them out, the excess moisture in the tortillas will vaporize when the tortillas hit the hot oil and cause the tortilla to puff up. That's not always a bad thing. In fact, you want the tortillas to puff when you're making something like gorditas, but when you want a flat tostada shell or corn chips, the puffiness can cause a problem.

For either tostadas or corn chips, begin with store-bought or homemade tortillas. Store-bought can work well, but you'll get the best flavor by following the recipe for Basic Corn Tortillas (page 25). If you are making corn chips, cut the tortillas into 8 triangles before drying them out. For either tostadas or corn chips, place the tortillas or tortilla triangles in the oven on a baking sheet at 350°F for 6 minutes or in a dry skillet over medium heat for 4 to 5 minutes.

Add about 1/2 inch corn or safflower oil to a medium-size (or large if you are making a lot chips or tostadas) pan and bring it to medium-high heat (375°F), about 4 to 5 minutes. Add the tortillas or triangles and fry them for 45 seconds to 1 minute per side until they are golden brown. The exact time will vary based on the thickness and moisture content of your tortillas.

Place the fried tortillas or chips on a wire rack or paper towel to drain. If you are making chips, immediately toss them with salt once they come out of the oil, or the salt will not stick to them very well.

Beans

If corn is king in Mexico, then the bean is queen. Together, beans and corn provide all the amino acids the human body needs. They formed the foundation of nutrition in the largely plant-based Mesoamerican societies. The common bean, which was first cultivated about seven thousand years ago in the Lerma-Santiago Basin of Mexico, includes pinto beans, kidney beans, navy beans, and black beans (among others).

Beans were so important they were used as a type of currency in the Aztec empire (along with other crops like cacao beans). Today, beans are one of the most successful crops on the planet, with an estimated 18.7 million tons produced annually. In Mexico, the bean's legacy as a primary food source remains intact. In the north, the pinto bean reigns supreme. In central Mexico, Peruvian beans and navy beans are popular choices, while black beans are the most popular bean everywhere else. Fava beans and garbanzo beans (a type of chickpea) are also frequently used. Whenever you sit down to eat in Mexico, chances are beans will make an appearance somewhere in the meal.

Following are recipes for popular staple bean dishes, like the classic Pot of Beans (page 29), which can be eaten as a meal on its own, used as one part of a more elaborate meal, or used as a component in other recipes. If you want to simply cook plain beans, the following tips will help you achieve the perfect bean: Use a water-to-bean ratio of about 5 parts water to 1 part dried beans, replenishing the water as needed. Skim away any of the bits that float. These are usually just skins, debris, or partially formed beans.

Bring the pot of dried beans to a boil, then reduce them to a simmer. Add about 1/2 teaspoon of salt for every 4 to 6 cups of water at the beginning of the cooking process. Salt will bump magnesium from the skin of the beans, making them more permeable, reducing the cook time, and flavoring the beans at the same time. Do not add acidic elements to the cooking liquid at the beginning as this will prolong the cook time. Epazote is often added as a flavoring agent and to help with some of the digestion problems that can occur with beans. Kombu can also be used to mitigate the digestive problems, but if you can find epazote, that should be your first choice. Soaking beans also aids with this.

Cook the beans until they are al dente, adding more salt (about 1/4 teaspoon for each 4 to 6 cups of water) about 15 minutes before they are done.

Fun Bean Fact

Refrito appears at first glance to mean refried (hence the English name for these beans), but Mexican Spanish often uses the prefix "re-" to mean "well" or "extra." In this case, refritos doesn't mean "refried," it simply means "well-fried."

Do not cook them to the point where they are splitting. Expect your beans to take anywhere from 45 minutes to 2 hours, depending on the size and age of the beans. Drain them, and they are ready for use. If you have leftover beans, you can freeze them and use them later.

Note that if you have old beans, they are still perfectly edible, but they'll take significantly longer to cook, sometimes twice as long as the cooking time for fresher beans. It's more important to pay attention to the changing texture of the beans as they cook than it is to cook them for a precise amount of time.

To Soak or Not to Soak

Soaking is not necessary prior to cooking the beans for the recipes in this book. Soaking does not appreciably accelerate the cooking time for beans, but if you soak your beans for about 12 hours, they'll begin the germination process, making them more digestible and increasing their nutrition profile. Soaking also reduces the amount of indigestible sugars found in beans, leeching some of those sugars into the water. If you do soak your beans, make sure you toss the soaking water, so you don't cook those sugars right back into the beans.

Mexican DIY

While you can find most ingredients at many markets, making your own can be extremely rewarding, especially when they're flavor powerhouses like the ones that follow. I use Garlic-Citrus Olive Oil (Mojo de Ajo, page 43) extensively in my cooking, and the Red Chorizo (page 40) can be subbed in (or even added as a main component to) many of the dishes in this book.

Pot of Beans
Frijoles de Olla

MAKES 6 CUPS

The quintessential pot of beans, frijoles de olla can be found simmering daily in most Mexican home kitchens. They are typically served directly from the cooking pot, usually an earthenware pot called an *olla de barro,* and they are served with the simmering broth. Beans are versatile, homey, tasty, and easy, and they get even better the next day. Frijoles de olla are often made with lard or bacon fat, so if you want a similar taste with your pot of beans, use the optional vegan shortening-liquid smoke-maple syrup mixture listed in the recipe.

1 pound dried beans (pinto, black, fava, garbanzo, or Peruvian), picked over, rinsed, and drained

10 cups water

1 small yellow or white onion, cut into 1/4-inch dice

1 1/2 to 2 teaspoons salt, divided

2 tablespoons vegan shortening + 1 tablespoon maple syrup + 1 teaspoon liquid smoke, combined, optional

3 to 4 tablespoons chile powder, optional (I prefer ancho powder with a dash of chipotle powder)

2 sprigs fresh epazote, chopped, or 1 tablespoon dried epazote, optional

Optional Garnishes:
1 Roma tomato, cut into 1/2-inch dice

1 small white onion, cut into 1/4-inch dice

1 serrano chile, seeded and minced

1/4 cup Roasted Chile Strips (page 39)

Add the beans, water, onion, 1/2 teaspoon of the salt, and optional shortening combination (if using) to a 4-quart pot and bring the water to a boil over high heat. Reduce the heat so that the water is simmering and cook until the beans are just soft. This will take 1 to 2 hours, depending on the size and age of the beans. Add the remaining 1 to 1 1/2 teaspoons salt and chile powder (if using), and cook until the broth is viscous, about 1 hour. If you are using the epazote, add it about 15 minutes before the beans are finished. Once the beans are served, add any of the optional garnishes.

Canned Beans

There's no shame in opening a can of beans instead of making some from scratch. I love a pot of home-cooked beans, but there are plenty of times I don't want to wait an hour or two to have them. If I want to infuse some flavor into those canned beans, I add my flavoring components, like chiles, onion, tomato, garlic, epazote, really any of the ingredients you'll see in the recipes in this section. Then I add 2 parts canned beans and 1 part water and simmer them until the water has evaporated. It's easy and usually done in about 10 minutes.

Refried Beans
Frijoles Refritos

MAKES 2 1/2 CUPS

Great refried beans require only a few components: well-flavored beans, a little extra chile flavor, some extra fat, and a good texture, one that is not completely smooth. I make a pot of Frijoles de Olla (Pot of Beans, page 29) as the base for my frijoles refritos when I have the time, but if I'm in a rush, I'll use leftover Frijoles de Olla or a couple cans of pinto beans so they can be ready in 20 minutes or so. For a low-fat version of this recipe, simply omit the shortening.

- 2 tablespoons vegetable shortening, optional
- 1 to 2 jalapeños or serrano chiles, stemmed, seeded, and halved lengthwise, or 2 chipotles in adobo
- 3 1/2 cups Frijoles de Olla (page 29) or 2 (15-ounce) cans pinto beans or black beans, undrained
- 1/4 teaspoon salt

Heat the shortening (if using) in a medium skillet over medium heat. Add the chiles and cook until the skins are almost blackened, 5 to 7 minutes. (If you are using chipotles in adobo instead of fresh chiles, do not add them to the skillet at this point.) Add the beans, chipotles in adobo (if using), and salt and bring to a simmer. Reduce the heat to medium-low and mash the beans using a potato masher, leaving some texture. Continue cooking, slowly stirring for about 10 minutes, or until the mashed beans thicken substantially, like a paste.

Drunken Beans
Pintos Borrachos

MAKES 4 1/2 CUPS

Pintos borrachos, or beans cooked with beer, is my favorite bean recipe. They're hearty, a little sweet, a little salty, and a lot delicious. The beer you use plays a large part in the flavor of these beans, so if you get a hoppy, bitter beer, your pintos borrachos will taste hoppy and bitter. That's why I use beers that feature dark malt as opposed to floral hoppiness.

- 1/4 cup vegan shortening, for creamier beans, optional
- 1 small yellow onion, cut into 1/4-inch dice
- 3 cloves garlic, minced
- 2 Roma tomatoes, coarsely chopped
- 4 cups water, plus more as needed
- 1 1/2 cups dried pinto beans
- 1/2 tablespoon dried epazote (optional, but recommended)
- 1 tablespoon dried Mexican oregano
- 3/4 teaspoon ground cumin
- 2 tablespoons Homemade Chile Powder (page 39)

1 (12-ounce) bottle dark ale or beer (try Samuel Smith's Nut Brown Ale)

3/4 teaspoon salt

If using the shortening, melt it over medium-high heat in a 3-quart pot or cazuela, then add the onion and sauté until it is lightly browned, about 5 minutes. Add the garlic and sauté 2 more minutes. Add the tomatoes, water, beans, epazote (if using), oregano, cumin, chile powder, ale, and salt and bring to a boil. (If you are not using the shortening, combine the onion, garlic, tomatoes, water, beans, epazote, oregano, cumin, chile powder, ale, and salt in the pot and bring to a boil over medium-high heat.)

Reduce the heat to medium-low and simmer until the beans are al dente, about 1 hour. If needed, add more liquid during this stage to keep the beans covered. Turn the heat up to high and bring the beans to a rapid boil, allowing the liquid to evaporate until the beans are stew-like, not soupy. Remove from the heat and mash the beans using a potato masher.

Make It Quick: If using the shortening, sauté the onion and garlic as above, then add 2 (15-ounce) undrained cans of pinto beans, along with the tomatoes, epazote, oregano, cumin, chile powder, ale, and salt. Simmer until the tomatoes have reduced and most of the liquid has cooked out of the pot, about 10 minutes. If you are not using the shortening, simply add everything to the pot at once, forgo sauteeing the onion, and bring to a simmer.

Oaxacan-Style Black Beans
Frijoles Negros Oaxaquenos

MAKES 6 1/2 CUPS

These beans are unique in that they are slow-cooked in the oven, creating a more dense texture than beans boiled in a pot of water. Ideally, they're cooked in an earthenware baking dish, which imparts a subtle flavor to the beans, but a glass baking dish will work just fine. What makes these beans really special is the aromatic undertones from avocado leaves and cinnamon. I can usually find dried avocado leaves at my local Mexican market, but if you don't have them, a pinch of fennel seeds will produce similar results.

1 pound dried black beans, picked over, rinsed, and drained

6 cups water

1 large yellow onion, cut into 1/4-inch dice

4 cloves garlic, halved lengthwise

2 whole dried ancho, mulato, or pasilla chiles

1 dried chipotle meco chile or 1 chipotle in adobo

1 tablespoon cumin seeds or 2 teaspoons ground cumin

1/2 teaspoon freshly cracked black pepper

1 (1-inch) cinnamon stick or 1/4 teaspoon ground cinnamon

2 avocado leaves or 1/4 teaspoon fennel seeds

1 teaspoon salt

Preheat the oven to 275°F. Combine the beans, water, onion, garlic, chiles, cumin, pepper, cinnamon stick or ground cinnamon, avocado leaves or fennel seeds, and salt in a 10 x 10-inch baking dish. Mix well, cover tightly with foil, and bake for 8 to 10 hours. Serve as is, or mash the beans before serving.

Rice

There was no rice in Mexico until the Spanish brought it to the port city of Veracruz in the 1520s. As rice is wont to do, it became an important part of the local cuisine. Central Mexico's warm, moist climate, perfect for growing rice, and its monsoon weather patterns, which create two growing seasons for rice, also played a large part in its further proliferation throughout the country. Today, rice is as much a part of the cocina as beans and squash. It's used as a side, as a paella-like dish, as part of a simple rice-and-beans dish, and is often added to soups to round them out. The rice dishes common throughout Mexican cooking are perfect examples of early Mexican-Spanish fusion cuisine.

Mexican rice is typically divided into two types, named after the regions in which they are commonly grown. Sinaloa is a long-grain rice and morelos is a short-grain rice. Arroz morelos, short-grain rice, is the most commonly used variety in Mexican dishes. However, short-grain rice also tends to be sticky, so it's usually lightly fried before being cooked (the oil keeps the pectin in the rice from causing the grains to stick together). To fry the rice, use 1 to 1 1/2 tablespoons of corn or olive oil for every 2 cups of dry rice and fry the dry rice over medium heat in a skillet for 5 to 7 minutes. If you don't want to fry your rice, use long-grain rice instead. And don't worry, you don't have to seek out morelos or sinaloa rice—any short-grain or long-grain rice will do.

Green Rice
Arroz Verde

MAKES 4 CUPS

Arroz verde is a refreshing, herbaceous alternative to Mexican red rice. I prefer serving it on a hot day, and it's a great side for lighter dishes. If you want to kick up the heat level, add a couple fresh serrano chiles. Serve with sliced avocado and lime wedges and a bowl of Oaxacan-Style Black Beans (page 31) for the perfect lunch.

- 2 poblano chiles, roasted
- 1 small white onion, coarsely chopped
- 4 bunches cilantro, stems included (3 cups, roughly chopped)
- 1/2 cup coursely chopped fresh epazote, optional
- 3 cloves garlic
- 3 cups vegetable broth, divided
- 1 teaspoon salt
- 2 tablespoons olive oil
- 1 1/2 cups medium-grain brown rice

In a blender or food processor, purée the poblanos, onion, cilantro, epazote (if using), garlic, 1 1/2 cups of the broth, and salt. Add the remaining 1 1/2 cups broth and blend well. Set the sauce aside.

In a medium saucepan, heat the oil over medium heat. Add the rice and toast it for 5 to 7 minutes, slowly stirring. Add the sauce and bring the mixture to a boil. Cover the pan, reduce the heat to low, and cook for 20 minutes.

Mexican Red Rice

Arroz Rojo Mexicano

MAKES ABOUT 6 CUPS

Mexican red rice is one of the original Mexican-Spanish fusion dishes. Based on the classic Spanish paella, Mexican red rice was born when native tomatoes replaced the far more expensive saffron. Like many Mexican rice dishes, the rice is lightly fried beforehand, giving the rice a toasty flavor and fluffiness. If you decide not to fry the rice, use long-grain rice instead of the medium-grain as the medium-grain is too sticky without frying.

- **2 large tomatoes or 4 Roma tomatoes**
- **2 1/2 cups vegetable broth**
- **1 1/2 tablespoons olive oil or vegetable oil**
- **1 large white onion, cut into 1/4-inch dice**
- **1 large carrot, cut into 1/4-inch dice**
- **2 cloves garlic, minced**
- **2 cups medium-grain brown rice**
- **1 1/2 teaspoons salt**
- **1 whole serrano or jalapeño chile**
- **1 dried bay leaf**
- **1/3 cup fresh or thawed frozen peas**

Purée the tomatoes and vegetable broth in a blender or food processor and set aside. For a smoother sauce, strain the tomato purée through a fine-meshed sieve to get rid of the pulp and seeds. In a large saucepan, heat the oil over medium-high heat. Add the onion and carrot and sauté for 4 to 5 minutes. Reduce the heat to medium. Add the garlic and sauté 1 minute. Add the rice and toast it, slowly stirring, for 5 to 7 minutes. Add the tomato purée, salt, serrano or jalapeño, and bay leaf. Bring the mixture to a simmer, cover, reduce the heat to low, and cook for 20 minutes. Remove from the heat, scatter the peas on top of the rice, and cover the pan again. Let the rice sit for 5 minutes, then fluff the rice and serve. Remove and discard the chile and bay leaf before serving.

Michoacán-Style Rice with Chorizo

Morisqueta con Chorizo

MAKES 3 3/4 CUPS

"Morisqueta" simply means "boiled rice." The word itself is a Spanish reference to the Moors, who ate boiled rice as a staple of their diet—and just like it was for the Moors, it's comfort food in Mexico. This particular recipe is a popular way to use leftover rice in Michoacán and Jalisco (and my house), combining it with sautéed onion, tomato, and chorizo. If you want something incredibly quick, you can also warm the rice and chorizo with your favorite salsa.

- **1 tablespoon olive oil**
- **1 small white onion, cut into 1/4-inch dice**
- **1 1/2 cups Red Chorizo (page 40) or store-bought vegan chorizo**
- **1 Roma tomato, coarsely chopped**
- **2 cups cooked rice (any kind)**

Salt, to taste

Fresh lime juice, optional

In a medium skillet, heat the oil over medium heat. Add the onion and sauté until it just starts to turn brown, 5 to 6 minutes. Add the chorizo and tomato and continue cooking until the tomato softens. Add the rice and salt, stirring to combine, and cook until the rice is warmed throughout. Add a squeeze of lime juice at the end, if you like.

Chiles

Chiles may not be in every Mexican dish, but it's rare that they're excluded from the party. Sometimes they're used just for heat—there are certainly plenty of extraordinarily hot chiles—but in most cases, the flavor of the chile should have preference over spiciness. A chile should add liveliness to a dish without killing the person eating it! OK, not always. For those of us that love dangerously spicy food and consider a habanero mild, spiciness is the highest priority, but we're also not like most people. For those of you who don't necessarily thrive on the hottest foods around, there are plenty of chiles that won't sear your taste buds. You can always adjust the heat level of a dish by decreasing or increasing the amount of chiles used.

If you need to tone down the heat of a chile, you can do so without reducing the chile flavor by removing the veins of the chile. Those are the whitish ridges holding the seeds that start from the stem end of the chile and run down the interior. The majority of the spiciness from a chile comes from those veins and, secondarily, the seeds. Use a small paring knife to remove the veins and seeds, and you'll get rid of much of the heat from the chile. Also, because those veins are condensed at the top of the chile, removing the top of the chile will remove a significant amount of heat. Finally, if you are sensitive to the capsaicin in chiles, you may find it beneficial to wear gloves when handling them so the capsaicin doesn't get on your hands.

You'll get the most out of your chiles by learning the techniques below, but I also urge you to pay attention to the type of chile being used. Chiles share a common basic flavor profile, but each type of chile has enough nuance to be noticeably different. A guajillo chile, for instance, tastes toasted and caramelized while an ancho chile, even though it is used in a similar way, will bring a fruity, caramelized flavor to your dishes.

Roasting Chiles

I love roasted chiles, especially chiles roasted over an open flame. Not only are they soft and lush, but there's a primal, charred element you get from the grill that you just don't get from the oven. You can roast just about any chile, even the tiny pequins. Regardless of the method you use, make sure to leave the chiles

Protect Your Skin and Eyes When Handling Chiles

Hot chiles contain a compound called capsaicin, which can burn your skin and eyes. Capsaicin will linger on your hands after handling chiles, and if you are handling very spicy chiles, a lot of it will linger. I've built an immunity to it, but for handling very hot chiles, I recommend using gloves and eye protection, especially if you are new to working with chiles. Even if you wear gloves, don't rub your eyes! You will have tears, but they will not be tears of joy. It's also very important to wash your hands thoroughly after handling chiles.

whole. As they roast, they'll steam on the inside and trapping that steam inside the chile makes the flesh of the chile nice and soft. With all of the methods, once both sides of the chiles are blackened, place them in a bowl and cover them with a towel. Wait about 10 minutes, until the chiles are cool enough to handle, then peel them and remove the seeds.

But don't be too fastidious about getting every single piece of blistered skin, as those blistered bits add a nice flavor to the chiles.

Open-Flame Roasting: Light a charcoal grill and place the chiles over the hottest part of the grill. As soon as the flesh blackens (you'll need to check the chiles every couple of minutes to see when this occurs), flip the chiles and blacken the other side. Don't let the chiles sit too long on the grill once the skin blackens. The goal is to blister the skin but not the flesh of the chiles. It typically takes 2 to 5 minutes to blacken one side of a chile, depending on the size of the chile and how hot your grill is. You can also roast chiles in a similar manner over the flame of a gas grill.

> ### Dry Your Chiles Completely!
> Make sure your chiles are very dry and not leathery. They should have very little give, if any. If the chiles are leathery, they will not grind into a powder, so you need to dry them further. Place them on a baking sheet or pizza stone and slowly bake them at 200°F until they are nearly brittle. The amount of time this will take depends on just how leathery your chiles are, but expect at least 30 minutes.

Pan-Roasting: Heat a heavy-bottomed pan, preferably an iron skillet or griddle, over medium heat. Place the chiles in the pan. Wait about 4 to 6 minutes before checking the chiles and make sure the undersides are mostly blistered. Once they are, flip the chiles and repeat. The flatter the chiles, the quicker they will roast.

Oven-Roasting: Preheat the oven to broil. If you are roasting large chiles, place the chiles directly on the top rack and cover the rack beneath it with foil. This will catch any juices that seep out of the roasting chiles and save cleanup time. If you are roasting small chiles, place them on a sheet of foil on the top rack. Broil them for 6 to 7 minutes, until the tops blister, then flip and repeat.

Toasting and Frying Dried Chiles

Toasting and frying dried chiles creates a more robust, but not necessarily spicier, flavor. It partially caramelizes the natural sugar found in chiles and activates their volatile compounds. That's a fancy way of saying it makes the chiles taste better. If you are toasting or frying a spicy dried chile, do so in a well-ventilated area. Once those chiles hit the pan, they'll start releasing capsaicin into the air. Capsaicin is the spicy compound in chiles and not something you want to breathe.

To toast the chiles, heat a dry pan over medium heat. If you are working with small chiles, like a chile de árbol or japone chile, toast them for about 10 seconds, quickly flip them in the pan or vigorously stir them so they turn over, and toast 5 more seconds. If you are toasting large chiles, like guajillo or ancho chiles, toast them for about 15 seconds per side.

Frying chiles will produce a deeper flavor than toasting them. To fry chiles, add about 1/2 inch of corn oil or safflower oil to a pan, heat it over just above medium heat, waiting about 5 minutes for the oil to properly heat. Make sure you have a fry basket or tongs and an easily accessible place to put the chiles. Carefully add the chiles to the oil. Small chiles take about 10 seconds total to fry and large chiles take about 5 to 10 seconds per side to fry. As soon as they are done, remove them from the oil and drain them on a paper towel or wire rack.

The key to getting the best flavor from toasting or frying your chiles is to make sure the chiles don't blacken. The chiles should turn a deeper hue of red, but not super dark. Once dried chiles blacken, they become bitter.

Rehydrating Dried Chiles

You'll get the most flavor out of your dried chiles by first placing them in a bowl, pouring steaming hot water over them, and letting them rehydrate for about 20 minutes. If you don't want to wait that long, you can simmer the chiles in a pot of boiling water, and they'll be done in 7 to 10 minutes. You lose a little flavor to the boiling water, but you save some time, too. Regardless of which method I use, I like to save the rehydrating water for use in making chile stocks, soups, stews, and even coffee. It's generally easier to remove the stems and seeds before rehydrating the chiles, unless the chile has one of those particularly hard-to-get-to stems, in which case, just pull out the stem and seed packet after the chile has rehydrated.

Drying Your Own Chiles

Making your own dried chiles is as simple as setting them out on your patio during the summer to dry. I live in Phoenix, where I get perfectly dried chiles in about four days. Make sure to keep them out of direct, prolonged exposure to the sun, or there is a good chance your chiles will get sun-bleached. If you don't live in a hot, arid climate (because you're sane), you can place your chiles on a baking stone or metal baking sheet on the absolute lowest temperature of your oven and dehydrate them, turning the chiles over halfway through the dehydration time. At 200°F, a jalapeño will take 8 to 12 hours and a poblano will take about 24 hours. If you have a dedicated dehydrator, you can also use that with the heat at the lowest setting. Similarly sized chiles will take a similar time to dry. If you grow your own chiles, you can let them dry directly on the plant. Store dehydrated chiles in a dry place and they can can last years. Don't seal them in a bag or jar since this will trap moisture.

Some of My Favorite Chile Powder Blends

While I love straight ancho powder, guajillo powder, or chipotle powder, I can't resist making my own blends. Here are some of my favorites:

- 10 guajillo chiles, 2 chipotles meco, and 2 teaspoons dark ground coffee
- 10 dried Hatch chiles and 1 tablespoon dried epazote
- 2 cups dried chiles de árbol, 1 tablespoon dried Mexican oregano, and 1/2 teaspoon garlic powder
- 4 ancho chiles, 4 mulato chiles, 4 guajillo chiles, 1 tablespoon burnt chile seeds, and 1/4 teaspoon smoked salt

Roasted Chile Strips
Rajas

MAKES 1 TO 1 1/2 CUPS

Rajas are often used as a garnish for tacos and other handheld foods like sopes and huaraches. They're not meant to add intense heat to a meal, but rather a lush chile flavor.

3 poblano, Hatch, Anaheim, or other large chiles, or 8 to 10 large jalapeños

Use one of the methods detailed on pages 35-37 to roast the chiles (an open flame will give you the best flavor and pan-roasting will give you the second best flavor). Once the chiles have cooled, peel away most of the skin, then remove the stems and seeds. Cut the chiles into strips about 2 inches long and 1/2-inch wide.

Homemade Chile Powder
Chiles Molidos

MAKES ABOUT 1/2 CUP

You can take any dried chile and turn it into your own homemade chile powder. Not only does the chile powder taste fresher, you can also make your own chile blends, allowing you to fine-tune the flavorings for your dishes. You'll probably find that you have to make more chile powder than you need simply because it's difficult for a blender to grind only one or two chiles at a time, so keep an airtight jar handy in which to store the leftover chile powder.

8 to 10 large dried chiles or 2 cups small dried chiles
1/8 teaspoon salt

Toast the chiles in a dry pan over medium heat for about 45 seconds. Remove the stems and seeds. Transfer the chiles to a blender (a blender will work better than a food processor here), add the salt, and slowly crank the speed of the blender up to high, blending until you have chile powder.

Pickled Onions or Chiles

Pickled veggies, especially onions and chiles, are common condiments found on tacos, tortas, and many antojitos. They're very easy to make and are ready to go in about 3 hours, though they get better the longer they sit. I often jar mine and keep them refrigerated. Once I use up the pickled ingredients, I simply slice more up and add them back to the jar with the vinegar to start another pickling batch.

For pickled onions, use red onions sliced paper thin. For pickled chiles, use jalapeños, serranos, and habaneros, as they are the most common. They should be sliced into rounds, not strips, and the seeds are sometimes removed from the habanero.

For the pickling liquid, choose a white vinegar. The less harsh the vinegar, the better the pickling. I like to use white balsamic to get some extra flavor into the veggies. If you want to flavor the pickling liquid, you can add fresh garlic, dried bay leaves, black peppercorns, whole cloves, a cinnamon stick, and Mexican oregano in any combination that you like.

Red Chorizo
Chorizo Rojo
MAKES 4 CUPS

Mexican chorizo is a ground sausage flavored with vinegar, chiles, and aromatic spices. It has a flavor reminiscent of both adobo and achiote paste. Unlike Spanish chorizo, which is a hard sausage, Mexican chorizo has a crumbly texture and uses chiles extravagantly. There are plenty of variations on the spice mix for chorizo, so feel free to play around with this recipe. The core elements are chiles, a little vinegar, and an aromatic spice, such as cinnamon, allspice, or cloves. Everything else is negotiable. Note that if you don't want to make your own, you may purchase ready-made vegan chorizo, available in natural food stores and well-stocked supermarkets.

Spice Mix and Marinade:
3 guajillo chiles or 3 tablespoons Homemade Chile Powder (page 39)

2 ancho chiles or 2 tablespoons ancho powder

1/2 tablespoon ground cumin

1 teaspoon ground coriander

1/2 teaspoon ground cinnamon

1/2 teaspoon ground allspice

1/2 teaspoon dried marjoram or Mexican oregano

1/3 teaspoon freshly ground black pepper

1/4 teaspoon ground cloves

2 tablespoons salt

1/4 teaspoon Indian black salt, optional

4 cloves garlic

1/4 cup olive oil or vegan shortening, optional

1/4 cup apple cider vinegar

1 teaspoon grated piloncillo or brown sugar

Chipotle powder or chile de árbol powder, to taste, optional

Sausage:
4 cups ground tempeh, ground seitan, TVP (textured vegetable protein),
 or ground dried mushrooms

In a dry skillet, toast the guajillo and ancho chiles for about 30 seconds on each side. Place them in a bowl large enough to hold the chiles. Bring a kettle of water to a boil. Pour the hot water over the chiles and let them rehydrate until they are soft. Remove the stems from the rehydrated chiles, but keep the seeds. Purée the chiles (or Homemade Chile Powder and ancho chile powder), cumin, coriander, cinnamon, allspice, marjoram, pepper, cloves, salt, black salt (if using), garlic, olive oil, vinegar, piloncillo, and chipotle powder (if using) in a blender or food processor. (Note that if you are using piloncillo instead of brown sugar, you will need to grate it with a microplane grater or other such implement. Also, the shortening will give the chorizo a fatty flavor while the olive oil will give it a smoother, cleaner flavor. Use whichever you prefer.)

(continues on page 42)

While the chiles are rehydrating, grind the tempeh, seitan, TVP, or dried mushrooms. Each protein works a little differently. See the following instructions for how to make them and how to use the Spice Mix and Marinade with them:

Tempeh: Place the tempeh in a food processor and pulse into very small crumbles. Only fill the food processor halfway and work in batches, if needed, so you don't end up with ground tempeh on top and tempeh paste on the bottom. The tempeh needs to sit in the marinade for a day to fully develop.

Seitan: If you are using store-bought seitan, treat it just like you would the tempeh. If you are making your own, you can cheat with this recipe by making the marinade and using it as the wet mix for your homemade seitan. This is a one-to-one replacement, so if you have one cup of marinade, you can replace one cup of liquid in your seitan. Save 1/4 cup of the Spice Mix and Marinade so you can toss your finished ground seitan in it to keep it moist. If you do it this way, your chorizo will be ready as soon as you grind your seitan.

TVP: Once you purée the Spice Mix and Marinade, add 2 cups of warm water to it and then toss the dehydrated TVP in it. It only takes about an hour for the TVP to fully absorb the chorizo flavoring and then it will be rehydrated and ready to use.

Ground Mushrooms: This version of the recipe is expensive, but incredibly good. You will need a molcajete or a mortar to make this (a food processor turns the mushrooms to powder too quickly). I typically use a mix of dried mushrooms, but you can use dried cremini, dried shiitake, or whatever else you have available. The dried cremini and shiitake will make the recipe much less expensive. If you use dried shiitakes, you will need about 8 cups of whole dried shiitakes. If you use other mushrooms, you will need about 12 cups. Working with a few mushrooms at a time, gently crush them in a molcajete into 1/4-inch pieces. The pieces don't need to be uniform, so don't worry about getting it perfect. Transfer the ground mushrooms to a large bowl and repeat until you have about 4 cups of crushed dried mushrooms. Add 1 cup of warm water to the marinade and pour it over the mushrooms. Toss immediately. After about 1 hour, the mushroom chorizo will be ready.

Make It Simple: Make a quick version by combining the chile and ancho powders, salt, and 1/4 cup of store-bought achiote paste combined with either 1/4 cup apple cider vinegar or fresh orange juice.

Simple Queso Fresco

Queso fresco is a common cheese used in a wide variety of Mexican dishes. It's sort of crumbly with a very slight sour note, and it's a little on the salty side. In my book *Vegan Tacos,* I explain how to make your own queso fresco from scratch. It's creamy and delicious and equally complex to make. It takes a time commitment and a willingness to experiment. Fortunately, I have discovered a simple hack for making a great vegan queso fresco. You'll need one tub of Kite Hill brand vegan ricotta. Crumble the ricotta onto cheese cloth or wax paper, making sure that the crumbles stay separated. Sprinkle 1/4 teaspoon salt all over the crumbles. Leave this out to dry for 6 hours and you have a queso fresco that surprisingly tastes and feels like the traditional dairy version.

Basic Guajillo Chile Sauce

MAKES ABOUT 1 1/2 CUPS

You can use this chile sauce to make enchiladas and chilaquiles, or smother tamales with it. You can also use it as a flavoring sauce for beans and rice, as a soup base, or simply to drizzle over a finished dish. If you don't use all of it in one sitting, place it in a jar and refrigerate. It will last a couple weeks. Also, feel free to substitute ancho chiles for any or all of the guajillo chiles to create a slightly sweeter sauce. For a tangy sauce, add the optional vinegar or lime juice.

6 guajillo chiles, 6 ancho chiles, or a mix, stemmed and rehydrated

1 cup reserved chile water

3 cloves garlic

1 teaspoon salt

1 teaspoon dried Mexican oregano or marjoram, optional

3 tablespoons distilled white vinegar or juice of 2 limes, optional

In a blender, purée the guajillo or ancho chiles, chile water, garlic, salt, oregano (if using), and vinegar (if using). Transfer the mixture to a small saucepan over medium heat, and gently simmer the sauce for 7 to 10 minutes.

Garlic-Citrus Olive Oil
Mojo de Ajo

MAKES 4 CUPS

Mojo de ajo is a roasted-garlic, citrus-infused oil that will make any taco pop with flavor. This is the secret weapon of Mexican cuisine. It's complex, rich, and zesty, and it's one of the essential ingredients of the Mexican kitchen. You can also make variations by flavoring it with different chiles. I always keep this kitchen treasure in my pantry, and if I start to run out, I make more.

4 cups olive oil

2 cups peeled whole garlic cloves (see note)

2 teaspoons coarse sea salt

1 cup fresh sour orange juice or lime juice

Preheat the oven to 325°F. Combine the oil, garlic, and salt in a large baking dish and roast for 45 minutes. Carefully remove the baking dish from the oven, stir the juice into the oil, and return it to the oven for another 20 minutes. Remove the baking dish from the oven again and mash the garlic using a potato masher or the back of a large, heavy spoon. Allow the mixture to cool and pour it into a jar with a mouth wide enough that you can reach in and spoon out some of the garlic bits. This will keep for up to 3 months at room temperature or up to 6 months if stored in a cool, dark place.

Note: For this recipe, I recommend using store-bought peeled garlic—it saves a lot of time.

SALSAS AND MORE

Salsas y Mas

I cannot think about Mexican food without thinking about salsa. A salsa brings all the components of a dish together. However, salsa shouldn't be thought of as a condiment.

Salsas can be used as cooking sauces, marinades, and even soup bases (after all, the word simply means "sauces"). I think there is a salsa for every occasion. Salsas can make or break a meal. If you decide to purchase a salsa instead of make your own, spend an extra dollar or two to get a good-quality salsa. Otherwise, all the work you put into your meal will be dragged down.

To make good-quality salsas, you'll want a blender and, ideally, a molcajete for crushing ingredients. Don't worry if you don't have a molcajete. It helps get the perfect texture, but you can get by with a solid bowl and a potato masher for crushing ingredients. You'll also want to develop your pan-roasting skills so you can get tomatoes, tomatillos, and garlic adequately charred and softened for the best flavor for your salsas. See page 18 for more information about pan-roasting.

In this chapter, I provide the basic salsas you should know, which are Pico de Gallo (also known as Salsa Mexicana, page 47), Salsa Verde (page 50), and the classic Crushed Red Salsa (page 48). I also include some other salsas that will take your meals to the next level, especially your antojitos. There are also some delicious dips, like a pumpkin seed dip called Sikil Pak (page 59), and a fried mashed zucchini dip that makes for interesting party food. Oh, and I didn't forget the guacamole!

If you want an extensive selection of more crazy-good salsas and hot sauces, check out *Vegan Tacos,* and for those of you who already have that book, this chapter features more buenas salsas de locos.

Pico de Gallo
Salsa Mexicana

MAKES 2 CUPS

You probably know salsa Mexicana by its other name, pico de gallo. This is the salsa my mom always made for parties or to go along with her enchiladas when I was growing up. As a child, I wouldn't have anything to do with it, but as an adult, I crave it. My mom's version uses salsa inglesa, also known as Worcestershire sauce, instead of lime juice. The key to this recipe is toning down the onions by rinsing them and using fresh, in-season tomatoes. The tomatoes will make or break this recipe. To create your own variations of pico de gallo, replace the tomatoes with 1 cup diced peaches, strawberries, apples, mango, pineapple, pickled chayote squash, cantaloupe, or peeled cucumber.

1/2 cup minced red onion, rinsed with cool water

3 Roma tomatoes, coarsely chopped

1 to 2 jalapeños, seeded and minced

1 clove garlic, minced

1/4 cup chopped fresh cilantro

Juice of 1 lime or 1 tablespoon salsa inglesa (vegan Worcestershire sauce)

Smash the onion two or three times in a molcajete or with a mortar and pestle. Add the tomatoes to the molcajete and crush them once or twice. You should still have mostly whole chunks of tomatoes. Stir in the jalapeños, garlic, cilantro, and lime juice, mixing until the ingredients are combined. Let the salsa rest for at least 10 minutes before serving to allow the flavors to meld.

Note: If you do not have a molcajete or mortar and pestle, simply cut the ingredients, combine them in a bowl, and allow them to rest for 15 minutes before serving.

Crushed Red Salsa
Salsa Roja de Molcajete

MAKES 2 CUPS

This is the classic crushed salsa. It has a robust sweetness from the roasted chiles, tomatoes, onions, and garlic and a nice rustic texture. A molcajete greatly speeds up the process of making this salsa, but you can easily make this in a mixing bowl with a potato masher or heavy wooden spoon.

> **3 Roma tomatoes, roasted**
> **2 jalapeños, roasted, or 2 chipotles in adobo**
> **1 medium white onion, cut into 3/4-inch thick discs**
> **4 cloves garlic**
> **3 tablespoons chopped fresh cilantro**
> **1/2 teaspoon salt**
> **Juice of 2 limes**

Preheat the oven to 450°F. Place the tomatoes and jalapeños in a baking dish and roast them for 15 minutes. (If you are using chipotles in adobo instead of jalapeños, you do not need to roast them, just the tomatoes.)

In a medium skillet over medium heat, pan-roast the onion and garlic until they are partially blackened. Chop the roasted onion and garlic and transfer them to a molcajete or mortar and pestle. When the tomatoes and jalapeños are done roasting, remove the stems from the jalapeños. Remove the seeds and veins if you want to tone down the heat.

Chop the jalapeños, but leave the tomatoes intact. You don't want to break the tomatoes until they are in the molcajete, so you can keep all the tomato juice in the salsa. Add the jalapeños, tomatoes, cilantro, salt, and lime juice to the molcajete and smash them to make a rough sauce. Give it a stir to make sure everything is evenly incorporated.

Tomato Habanero Salsa
Chiltomate

MAKES ABOUT 1 CUP

Chiltomate is a smooth roasted tomato and chile salsa. The salsa is actually cooked twice, once when the tomatoes and chile are roasted, and again when the salsa is fried, further caramelizing it and deepening its flavor. You can use any sort of chile, but habaneros are the most popular. Use two if you want the salsa particularly spicy. You can use this as a dipping salsa, a salsa for tacos and tostadas, or even as a pasta sauce.

4 Roma tomatoes
1 to 2 habanero chiles
1 clove garlic
1/2 small white onion, roughly chopped
1 teaspoon salt
2 tablespoons olive oil

Preheat the oven to 500°F. Place the tomatoes and habaneros in a small baking dish lined with parchment paper and roast them for 10 minutes. Transfer them to a blender, add the garlic, onion, and salt, and purée until smooth. Heat the oil in a small pot at just above medium heat. Add the sauce, pressing through a strainer if you want the smoothest texture, and cook the sauce for 10 minutes, stirring occasionally.

Peach Serrano Salsa
Salsa de Durazno y Chile Serrano

MAKES 1 1/4 TO 1 1/2 CUPS

This is a simple fresh salsa that marries two of my favorite elements, sweet and spicy. You can use this as a dip or as a sweet topping to lighten heavier dishes. Because all the elements are fresh and there are so few of them, you must make sure to get high-quality, in-season produce. My favorite peaches to use are white peaches for their pure taste. Whenever they come in season, this salsa is one of the first things I make.

3 medium, sweet peaches cut into 1/4-inch dice
1 to 2 serrano chiles, seeded and minced
1/4 teaspoon salt
Juice of 1 lime
1 tablespoon minced fresh cilantro or epazote

Smash the peaches in a molcajete or bowl. Stir in the serranos, salt, lime juice, and cilantro or epazote.

Salsa Verde
Salsa Verde Cocida

MAKES 4 CUPS

This is a simple cooked salsa verde. Cooking the tomatillos removes much of their tartness and sweetens the overall salsa. It's great not only for tacos but it's also perfect for jarring and for setting out as a dip for chips.

- 5 poblano chiles, pan-roasted, stems removed and discarded
- 8 large tomatillos, husks removed and finely chopped
- 1/2 medium yellow onion, minced (a little less than 1/2 cup)
- 2 cloves garlic, minced
- 2 cups chopped fresh cilantro
- 1/4 cup chopped fresh epazote (optional, but recommended)
- 3/4 teaspoon salt
- 1/4 cup water

Coarsely chop the pan-roasted poblanos and set them aside. In a 2-quart saucepan over medium heat, combine the tomatillos, onion, garlic, cilantro, epazote (if using), salt, and water and simmer for 7 to 8 minutes. As the tomatillos soften, press on them with a heavy wooden spoon or potato masher to release more of their juices. Add the reserved poblanos to the saucepan and simmer 2 minutes longer.

Olive and Tomato Salsa
Salsa Veracruzana

MAKES ABOUT 2 CUPS

This salsa is the perfect marriage between Mexican and Spanish cuisines, a blend of chiles and tomatoes spiked with olives and capers. This isn't just a dipping salsa. It can be used as a sauce for grilled veggies, and it can be thinned out with a little water and extra tomatoes to make a soup base. With the addition of potatoes, almonds, and fishless fillets or oyster mushrooms, you can turn this into a vegan version of Veracruz's famous bacalao, which is normally made with cod (see Fish-Free Bacalao, page 179).

> 1 tablespoon olive oil
> 1/2 medium white onion, minced
> 2 cloves garlic, minced
> 2 banana chiles (preferably pickled), seeded and cut into 1/4-inch dice
> 5 Roma tomatoes, cut into 1/2-inch dice
> 10 to 12 pitted brine-cured green olives (preferably stuffed with garlic), thinly sliced
> 3 tablespoons capers
> 1 teaspoon minced fresh oregano
> 3/4 teaspoon salt

Heat the oil in a large skillet over medium heat. Add the onion and sauté until it is slightly browned, about 6 minutes. Add the garlic and sauté 2 more minutes. Add the banana chiles, tomatoes, green olives, capers, oregano, and salt and simmer for 5 to 10 minutes, until the tomatoes have reduced to a chunky sauce.

Burnt Chipotle Salsa
Salsa de Chipotle Quemado

MAKES ABOUT 1 CUP

This salsa has a deep, robust, bitter flavor created by charring chipotles and combining them with sweet and sour ingredients. It's intense as a dipping salsa, but really shines with grilled foods and with albóndigas (Mexican Meatballs in Serrano Tomato Sauce, page 166).

- 3 tablespoons corn oil
- 6 chipotles meco
- 1 small white onion, cut into 1/4-inch dice
- 4 cloves garlic, smashed
- 1/2 teaspoon cumin seeds
- 2 Roma tomatoes, coarsely chopped (optional)
- 2 tablespoons agave syrup
- Juice of 1 lime
- 1 teaspoon salt

Heat the oil in a small skillet over medium heat. Add the chipotles and fry them until blackened on both sides. Remove them from the oil and transfer them to a blender. Add the onion to the oil and sauté until well browned, about 8 to 10 minutes. Add the garlic and sauté 3 minutes. Add the cumin seeds and sauté 1 minute. Add the tomatoes (if using) and cook 5 minutes. Transfer the chipotles, onion, garlic, tomatoes, cumin seeds, agave, lime juice, and salt to a blender and purée until smooth.

Cocida y Cruda (Cooked and Raw)

Salsas crudas are salsas made with fresh, uncooked ingredients, and salsas cocidas are salsas made with cooked ingredients.

Guacamole

At its purest, guacamole is simply mashed avocado, lime, and salt. Everything else is negotiable. However, that doesn't mean there aren't plenty of variations on the theme. I like to think of the Basic Guacamole as a template to which I can add different flavors and textures with a few simple additions. Guacamole is best made in a molcajete. It's designed for making dishes like guacamole and the presentation is beautiful. Following are some ideas for spicing up your guacamole. Each of these uses the Basic Guacamole recipe and the instructions tell you how to incorporate the different ingredients.

Basic Guacamole

MAKES ABOUT 1 CUP

2 ripe Hass avocados, pitted and peeled
Juice of 2 limes
1/3 teaspoon salt

In a bowl or molcajete, combine the avocados, lime juice, and salt. Mash to combine, but don't make the guacamole completely smooth.

Variations

Pepita-Pomegranate Guacamole

3 tablespoons pomegranate seeds
2 tablespoons salted roasted pepitas

Add the pomegranate seeds and pepitas to the top of the Basic Guacamole after it has been made.

Roasted Garlic–Poblano Guacamole

1 poblano chile, roasted, stemmed and seeded
6 cloves roasted garlic

Mash the poblano and garlic into a paste and stir it into the Basic Guacamole.

Mango-Cilantro Guacamole

1/4 cup diced mango
3 tablespoons minced red onion, rinsed with cool water
2 tablespoons minced fresh cilantro

Stir the mango, onion, and cilantro into the Basic Guacamole once it's been made.

Tomatillo and Pine Nut Guacamole

1 raw tomatillo, cut into 1/4-inch dice
1 serrano chile, seeded and minced
1 tablespoon toasted pine nuts

Stir the tomatillo, serrano, and pine nuts into the Basic Guacamole.

Squash Dip
Calabacitas Fritas

MAKES ABOUT 2 1/4 CUPS

This is a specialty of Yucatán that can be used as a dip, sauce, or soup. I also like serving it on tostadas. It's basically zucchini and a Caribbean sofrito redolent with aromatic spices like allspice, cloves, and black pepper. It's one of those dishes that's better the next day, but I rarely have the patience to wait that long. Because this dish relies so heavily upon the spices, it's best if you toast whole spices and then grind them before using them in the recipe. Serve this with chips or sliced raw zucchini.

- 4 whole cloves or 1/8 teaspoon ground cloves
- 4 allspice berries or 1/8 teaspoon ground allspice
- 6 black peppercorns or 1/4 teaspoon ground black pepper
- 1 teaspoon dried Mexican oregano or marjoram
- 1 dried bay leaf
- 2 tablespoons olive oil
- 2 medium zucchini or Mexican gray squash, coarsely chopped
- 1/2 cup fresh or frozen corn kernels
- 1 small white onion, cut into 1/4-inch dice
- 4 cloves garlic, minced
- 3/4 teaspoon salt
- 2 small Roma tomatoes, coarsely chopped
- 2 serrano chiles, seeded and minced
- 2 tablespoons chopped fresh cilantro, for garnish

If you are using ground cloves, allspice, and pepper, do not toast them. Otherwise, toast the whole cloves, allspice berries, and peppercorns in a medium dry skillet over medium heat for 2 minutes, slowly stirring. Remove the spices from the skillet and finely grind them in a molcajete, a spice grinder, or a blender. The oregano and bay leaf do not need to be ground.

In the same skillet, heat the oil over medium heat. Add the zucchini and sauté for 7 to 8 minutes, until lightly browned. Transfer the zucchini to a bowl and coarsely mash.

Return the skillet to the heat. Add the corn and sauté for 5 minutes. Add the onion and sauté 6 to 7 minutes. Add the garlic and sauté 2 minutes. Add the salt, tomatoes, serranos, ground spice mixture, oregano, and bay leaf. As soon as the tomatoes soften, add the mashed zucchini. Cook until most of the liquid has evaporated and the mixture thickens. Remove from the heat, transfer to a serving plate, and garnish with the cilantro.

Pumpkin Seed Dip
Sikil Pak

MAKES 1 3/4 CUPS

Sikil pak is a centuries-old Mayan pumpkin seed dip recipe popular in Yucatán, but in modern restaurants, it's the rising star, replacing artisan guacamole as the haute cuisine Mexican dip. I don't care where it's served, in fancy restaurants or on the street, I will eat an entire bowl of sikil pak in a couple minutes if you let me. It's the heady creaminess of the pumpkin seeds combined with the slightly sweet, slightly tart roasted tomatillos that pulls me in. Serve with tortillas, tortilla chips, or sliced raw squash.

4 large tomatillos, husks removed
1/2 small white onion, cut into 1/4-inch thick rings
3 cloves garlic, unpeeled
1 cup unsalted raw pepitas
1 teaspoon salt
1/4 cup loosely packed fresh cilantro

Heat a skillet (preferably cast iron) over medium heat. Place the tomatillos, onion, and garlic in the skillet. As the tomatillos and onion rings blister and the garlic paper becomes dark brown, flip the ingredients and repeat. The garlic and onion will finish after 7 to 8 minutes and the tomatillos after 12 to 15 minutes. Place the tomatillos, onion, garlic, pepitas, salt, and cilantro in a blender and purée until completely smooth.

Chef's Tip: For a better texture, grind the ingredients in a molcajete, starting with the onion, garlic, and salt until they become a rough paste. Next, add the pepitas and cilantro and continue smashing until the pepitas are creamy. Finish with the tomatillos, smashing them into the creamy pepitas until the Sikil Pak is mostly smooth. It's a lot more effort, but you will be well rewarded.

STREET FOOD

Antojitos

Antojitos are quintessential Mexican street food, and like most things Mexican, defy hard-and-fast definitions. Typically, antojitos are dishes that aren't eaten at formal, sit-down meals.

The "little cravings" known as antojitos are quick to serve, quick to eat, and form the basis of most street food. It's impossible to talk about street food without talking about antojitos, and it's impossible to talk about Mexican food without talking about street food. That's because in Mexico, food is life and the street is where you find its vibrant, pulsating beat. The puestas and fondas (food stalls and open-air restaurants) that crowd so many plazas and bus stops are where much of the creativity in the Mexican food scene is currently happening, with new, spectacular dishes being created every day. And more vegan-friendly places are popping up, especially in Mexico City.

Even in high-end restaurants, elevated street food can be found on the menu. Chefs from all over the world come to Mexico to find inspiration from these lively foods. There is a burgeoning food-truck and street-food movement in the United States, where some of the best chefs in the country are serving delicious, hip foods from the window of a truck—but the street-food scene in Mexico is the granddaddy of them all. It's the far hipper granddad that still goes out dancing and drinking every night, smokes the best cigars, and manages to be the life of the party no matter how old he is. If that sounds a little sensational, you'll have to forgive me, because the street food in Mexico is nothing less than sensational.

Antojitos aren't only street food, even though that's where they are most commonly eaten. They can also be found in restaurants and home cocinas. Sometimes home food and street food become interchangeable. The most common antojitos are made from masa and include some foods you probably recognize, like tacos, tostadas, tamales, and enchiladas, and some foods you might not recognize like the oblong-shaped huaraches, the sweet potato and masa cakes called garnachas, and stuffed black bean masa cakes called bocoles. They also include an entire category of sandwiches called tortas, snacks like chile and lime–dressed fruit, and even some soups like pozole. As long as they're easy to serve and informal, they're probably an antojito.

Because I have sections devoted exclusively to tacos, enchiladas, and other similar popular foods, this first section is more of a catch-all of the other popular antojitos: quesadillas, gorditas, and snacks. The antojitos in this section are eminently versatile. You'll see filling or topping ideas to go with each type of antojito, but those are just suggestions. You can take just about any of the toppings, fillings, and sauces found throughout the book and mix and match them onto the different antojitos. Want to top your garnachas with the potatoes-and-beans topping from the Potato and Drunken Bean Gorditas (page 72) or top your tostadas with the lentil tinga from the Sweet Potato Corn Cakes (page 70)? Do it! Have fun with them and make them yours. Those are the most authentic antojitos of them all.

Mercado de Antojitos

Antojitos are so vital to the food world in Mexico, there are two entire markets dedicated just to them, both called *Mercado de Antojitos*, located in Coyoacán, and another one in Uruapan, Michoacán. Both offer a number of vegan options, and it's a fun foodie trip if you're in the area.

Mexican Street Corn and Street Corn Salad
Elotes y Esquites

MAKES 4 SERVINGS

Nothing captures the essence of street food in Mexico more than classic elotes. If there is a group of food stalls around, chances are at least one of them is selling this miracle of whole corn slathered in mayo and salty cheese, dressed with a sprinkling of chile powder and lime. They're also a popular home treat, simply because they are easy to make and they pop with flavor. You can take the easy route with this one and do the boiled version, but the grilled version is simply divine. Esquites is a delicious variation of elotes, simply served in salad form.

- 4 fresh ears corn
- 1/2 cup vegan mayonnaise
- 1/4 teaspoon coarse sea salt
- 1 cup crumbled Simple Queso Fresco (page 42) or your choice of crumbly vegan cheese
- 2 teaspoons Homemade Chile Powder (page 39) or chile powder of your choice
- 3 tablespoons minced fresh cilantro
- 1 lime, cut into 4 wedges

Boiled Corn: Leave the corn ears in their husks and cut the silk away from the top of the corn. Bring a pot of water to a boil in a pot big enough to submerge the corn. Add 1 tablespoon of salt to the pot. Add the corn ears to the pot and boil them for 5 minutes. Remove the corn ears from the pot and let them cool. Peel back the husks to use as a handle.

Grilled Corn: If you are using a charcoal or wood grill, let the flames die down and allow the coals to get very hot. If you are using a gas grill, the heat should be medium-high. Remove the husks from the corn ears. Grill the corn until partially blackened all the way around the cob. The time will vary based on exactly how hot your grill is and how close your grill rack is to the hot coals. Remove the corn and allow it to cool. Skewer the corn to create a handle.

Dressing: Combine the mayonnaise, salt, and cheese. Slather this on each ear of cooked corn. Dress each ear with about 1/2 teaspoon of guajillo chile powder and 3/4 teaspoon minced cilantro. Serve with the lime wedges.

Corn Salad (Esquites): Cook the corn ears using one of the methods above, then cut off the kernels and discard the cobs. Alternatively, you can sauté 4 cups of corn kernels over medium-high heat in 1 tablespoon of oil until the kernels brown. Toss the cooked kernels with the mayonnaise, salt, Simple Queso Fresco, and chile powder. Serve with lime wedges on the side.

Veracruz-Style Empanadas
Empanadas Veracruzanas

MAKES 10 EMPANADAS

I nearly always think of empanadas as part of a tapas plate, but there are some outstanding ones served in Mexico, each with its own regional twist and nearly all of them made with corn dough instead of wheat. The ones served in Veracruz are my favorite, closely marrying Spanish elements like raisins, capers, and olives with Mexican ingredients like corn and chiles for little handheld flavor bombs that always entice me to eat way more of the little fried corn pockets than I should!

1 tablespoon olive oil
1/4 cup finely chopped onion
3/4 cup slivered almonds
3 Roma tomatoes, seeded and coarsely chopped
3 cloves garlic, minced
4 pitted brine-cured green olives, finely chopped
1 tablespoon capers
3/4 teaspoon minced fresh rosemary
1 serrano chile, seeded and minced
1 tablespoon raisins
1/4 teaspoon salt
1/4 teaspoon freshly ground black pepper
1 tablespoon minced fresh parsley
1 cup prepared masa
Corn oil
Your favorite salsa, for serving

Filling: Heat the oil in a medium skillet over medium heat. Sauté the onion in the oil for 10 minutes, until it is well caramelized. Add the almonds, tomatoes, garlic, green olives, capers, rosemary, serrano, raisins, salt, and pepper to the skillet and cook 5 minutes. Remove the skillet from the heat and immediately stir in the parsley.

Empanadas: Fill a medium skillet with about 1 1/2 inches of corn oil and heat it to medium-high heat. The oil should be hot, but not smoking.

Roll the prepared masa into 10 balls, each about 1 1/4 inches in diameter. Cover them with plastic wrap to keep them from drying out. Using a tortilla press, press each one into a tortilla 4 inches in diameter. Alternatively, you can place them between two sheets of wax paper and flatten them with your palm or a heavy pan into tortillas. Fill each mini-tortilla with 1 tablespoon of filling, fold it in half, and pinch it closed. Fry each one about 1 minute per side, then set on a paper towel to cool and drain. These are best if eaten within a few minutes of coming out of the oil. Serve with salsa.

Northern Mexico Chimichangas
Chivichangas del Norte

MAKES 4 CHIMICHANGAS

Chimichangas, called chivichangas in Mexico, are basically deep-fried burritos. A little decadent, but wonderful as an occasional treat. I found these everywhere on the streets of Nogales and Sonoita when I traveled through the border towns, rolled right on the spot and deep fried in large pots of hot corn oil. They epitomize the mingling of the American-Mexican border culture by their use of flour tortillas mixed with a filling suffused with adobo. You can find these in Tucson as easily as on the Sonoran side of Nogales. I provide several variations on the chimichanga, and you should feel free to create your own.

1 teaspoon corn oil, plus more for frying
1 cactus paddle or large zucchini, trimmed and cut into 3/4-inch dice
Pinch salt
1 cup shredded seitan or 1 large portobello mushroom, cut into 1/4-inch dice
1/4 cup adobo sauce from 1 (7-ounce) can chipotles in adobo
4 burrito-size flour tortillas
1 cup Refried Beans (page 30) or store-bought refried beans
1 cup shredded lettuce
Salsa of your choice

Heat the oil in a medium skillet over high heat. Add the cactus paddle or zucchini and salt to the skillet, and cook for 7 to 8 minutes. Set aside. Toss the seitan or portobello in the adobo and set aside.

Add enough oil to a deep fryer or Dutch oven to cover a burrito by 1 to 2 inches and bring it to 375°F. Along the left side of a tortilla, spread 1/4 cup of the Refried Beans, leaving about 2 inches uncovered on both the bottom and top of the tortilla. Place 1/4 cup of the seitan or portobello on top of the beans, followed by 2 to 3 tablespoons of cactus. Roll the tortilla closed about halfway. Fold the top and bottom of the tortilla inward, then tightly roll the rest of the tortilla closed, tucking the top and bottom folds into the tortilla as you roll it, making a burrito. Repeat this with the remainder of the filling and tortillas.

Working one at a time, add a burrito to the hot oil, holding it closed with tongs, and fry it for 2 minutes. Remove from the heat and transfer to a paper towel to drain. Repeat with the remaining burritos. Serve with shredded lettuce and your favorite salsa.

Other Filling Ideas (use these as additions or in place of other ingredients as you see fit):

- 1 1/2 cups smashed cooked beans
- 1/2 cup shredded vegan cheese
- 2 tablespoons Mexican oregano
- 1 large zucchini, cut into 1/2-inch dice
- 1 cup Red Chorizo (page 40)
- 1/2 cup cooked black beans

Sopes with Smashed Charro Beans and Fried Chiles

Sopes de Frijoles Charros Machacados y Chiles Fritos

MAKES 10 SOPES

A sope is a super-thick tortilla with pinched-up sides that holds a mound of filling. Beans and salsa are by far the most common fillings, but because of its popularity all across Mexico, there are hundreds of regional varieties. In fact, some of the other antojito recipes in this book are really just regional variations of the sope. Other popular toppings include chopped onion, queso fresco, chorizo, grilled squash, fresh squash blossoms, shredded lettuce, and pickled habaneros. While sopes can be fried, I much prefer the version that comes straight off the hot comal. It's simple, primal, and absolutely delicious. Think of a sope as a thick tostada and let your imagination go wild. (Note that if you don't want to make your own sopes, many Mexican markets sell them premade.)

Sopes:
1 cup Homemade Masa (page 23) or 6 store-bought sopes

Filling:
1 1/2 cups smashed Pot of Beans (page 29) or refried beans of your choice
1 cup Guacamole (page 56)
15 to 20 Pickled Onions (page 39), separated into rings
16 to 20 fried chiles de árbol

Heat a comal or griddle over medium heat. Divide the masa into 10 balls, keeping them covered with a slightly damp towel or plastic to prevent them from drying out. Line each plate of a tortilla press with plastic and place one of the masa balls on the press. Gently press the masa, but don't push all the way down. The tortilla should be thick and about 3 1/2 to 4 inches in diameter. Repeat this with the remaining masa balls, making sure to keep them covered once pressed.

Place a sope onto the comal or griddle and cook it for 2 minutes. Flip it and cook it 1 more minute. Keep the sope on the heat and, using your fingers, form a rim about 1/3-inch high. Once the rim is formed, remove the sope from the heat and repeat this with the remaining sopes. If you do not feel comfortable working the sope with your fingers while it is cooking, cook the second side for 1 minute. Transfer it to a plate and form the rim, then transfer it back to the comal or griddle and cook it 1 more minute. Spread the sopes with the smashed Charro Beans and Guacamole, then add the Pickled Onions and fried chiles de árbol.

Tone Down the Heat: Skip the chiles de árbol, or toast an ancho chile, crush it, and sprinkle about 1/4 teaspoon of it over each sope. That way, you still get the chile flavor without all the heat of the chiles de árbol.

Other Filling Ideas:

- Basic Guajillo Chile Sauce (page 43), roasted garlic, and Simple Queso Fresco (page 42) or toasted pine nuts
- Oaxacan-Style Black Beans (page 31), minced onion, and diced fresh tomato
- Red Chorizo (page 40), potatoes, and strips of roasted poblano

- Beans, Burnt Chipotle Salsa (page 54), pickled cabbage, mole negro, Guacamole (page 56), and toasted pine nuts
- Shredded lettuce, tomato, avocado, shredded seitan, Pickled Onions (page 39), and lime wedges

Sope

Sweet Potato Corn Cakes with Lentil Tinga
Garnachas Camotes de Tinga de Lentejas

MAKES 8 GARNACHAS

I have a fondness for all the different masa-based antojitos, but garnachas are at the top of the list. They're a thick corn and sweet potato cake, lightly fried or baked, and topped with a host of different toppings. In this case, I top mine with a Lentil Tinga, my version of the famous tinga dishes from Puebla, Mexico. Tingas are a spicy, heady mix of tomatoes, onion, and chipotles in adobo and they balance the sweetness of the garnachas perfectly.

Lentil Tinga:
2 tablespoons olive oil
1 large white onion, sliced paper thin
3 cloves garlic, minced
4 large Roma tomatoes, coarsely chopped
1 to 2 chipotles in adobo, finely chopped, plus 2 tablespoons of adobo
    sauce
1 teaspoon salt
1 tablespoon apple cider vinegar
1 1/4 cups water
3/4 cup brown lentils, picked over, rinsed, and drained

Garnachas:
1 medium white sweet potato, about 12 ounces (see note)
1 1/2 cups Homemade Masa (page 23)
Corn oil, for frying
Chopped fresh cilantro, for serving

Lentil Tinga: Heat the oil in a 2-quart pot over medium heat. Add the onion and cook until it is lightly browned, about 5 minutes. Add the garlic and sauté 1 minute. Add the tomatoes, chipotles, salt, and apple cider vinegar and cook until the tomatoes reduce to a thick sauce. Add the water and bring the mixture to a simmer. Add the lentils, stir, and bring the mixture back to a simmer. Cover the pot, reduce the heat to low, and cook for 17 to 20 minutes, until the lentils are al dente. Set the lentils aside and keep them warm.

Garnachas: Preheat the oven to 450°F. Wrap the sweet potato in foil, place it in a baking dish large enough for the sweet potato to fit in and roast the sweet potato about 45 minutes, until you can pierce it with a fork all the way to the center. Remove it from the oven, unwrap it, and peel it once it is cool enough to handle. Add 2 inches of corn oil to a medium heavy-bottomed pan and heat it to 375°F.

While the oil is heating, mash the sweet potato and, working by hand, thoroughly combine it with the Homemade Masa. Separate the sweet potato dough into 8 balls and cover them with a moist towel so they don't dry out. Using your palms, flatten the balls into palm-size ovals. Pinch a small edge around each oval, about 1/3-inch high, turning each of the ovals into a small-rimmed boat (these are your garnachas).

Cover them again as you finish patting each one out.

Fry each of the garnachas in the heated corn oil for 2 to 3 minutes, until they are crispy and golden. Remove them and set them aside on a paper towel to drain. Fill them with 1/2 cup of filling of your choice, and cover each with about 3 tablespoons of the Lentil Tinga, garnish with the cilantro, and serve.

Note: The key to these garnachas is using a white sweet potato for its smooth, pure flavor. If you can't find white sweet potatoes, simply use 2 cups masa instead.

Chef's Tip: Don't worry if your sweet potato is heavier than 3/4 pound. It is more important that it roasts whole. Once it roasts, measure out the 3/4 pound and save the excess for another dish.

Chef's Tip: Reserve a small bit of masa, about a 1/2-inch ball, to test the oil. Place the bit of masa in the oil and if it crisps and turns golden brown, your oil is ready. If it doesn't, wait another few minutes for it to properly heat.

Make Them Low-Fat: Instead of frying the garnachas, place them on a silicone mat and bake them at 350°F, uncovered, for 20 minutes.

Fruit with Chile Powder and Lime
Fruta con Chile Molido y Limón

MAKES 1 SERVING

A quick snack ubiquitous across Mexico, this simple dish of sweet fruit, tart lime, salt, and chile powder is sure to perk up your day. Use whatever fruit or melons are in season and choose a chile powder appropriate for your heat tolerance. I prefer pequín chile powder, but if you don't like it spicy, you can use a mild chile powder (like ancho or guajillo) or powder made from mild California or New Mexico chile pods. The fruit is usually served in cups and occasionally comes with hot sauce on the side.

> 2 cups sliced fruit such as mango, pineapple, watermelon, cantaloupe, co-
> conut, or peaches
> 1/2 teaspoon salt
> Juice of 2 limes
> 1 to 2 teaspoons chile powder of your choice
> Hot sauce, optional, for serving

Toss the fruit, salt, lime juice, and chile powder together and serve immediately with the hot sauce (if using). You can also dehydrate the dressed fruit until it is leathery to have spicy, salty fruit leather.

Potato and Drunken Bean Gorditas
Gorditas de Papas y Frijoles Borrachos

MAKES 10 GORDITAS

Gorditas ("little fat ones") are the ultimate street food. These stuffed corn cakes are the perfect handheld treat. They have just enough substance to bring me to the edge of being satisfied and plenty of flavor to entice me back for more. As one of the more versatile antojitos, they can be stuffed with just about any filling imaginable. One of my favorites is a simple mix of potatoes, beans, and chiles, but I also love gorditas stuffed with chorizo, cactus, or chopped grilled veggies. I've even made a version with grilled peaches and chiles de árbol that turned out spectacularly well. Feel free to use any filling you like. Try some of the fillings from other recipes in this book. You will not be disappointed.

Filling:
3 guajillo chiles, rehydrated
2 cloves garlic
1/4 teaspoon salt
1 tablespoon corn oil or Garlic-Citrus Olive Oil (page 43)
3 medium red potatoes, cut into 1/4-inch pieces

Gorditas:
1 cup masa harina
1/2 cup unbleached all-purpose flour
1/2 teaspoon salt
1/2 teaspoon baking powder
1 1/2 cups warm water
Corn oil, for frying
1 1/2 cups mashed Drunken Beans (page 30) or mashed black beans
1/4 cup chopped fresh cilantro or epazote

Filling: Purée the guajillos, garlic, and salt in a blender or food processor and set aside. Heat the oil in a medium skillet over medium-high heat, and fry the potatoes until they are lightly browned, about 7 to 8 minutes. Reduce the heat to medium. Add the chile purée, bring to a simmer, and cook 1 more minute. Turn the heat to low to keep the potatoes warm while you make the gorditas.

Gorditas: Bring a griddle to medium heat. Combine the masa harina, flour, salt, and baking powder in a mixing bowl at least 4 cups in size. Add the water and mix by hand until you have a supple dough. Divide the dough into 10 equal portions, roll them into balls, and cover them with plastic or a slightly damp cloth to keep them from drying out. Cover each plate of a tortilla press with plastic wrap. Place a masa ball in the center of the press, just slightly toward the hinge. Press the masa until it is about 1/4-inch thick and about 4 inches in diameter. Transfer this to the griddle and cook it for about 1 1/2 minutes on each side. Repeat this process until you have cooked all the gorditas. Set aside.

Add about 1/2 inch of oil to a medium skillet and heat it to 350°F. Fry each gordita for 15 to 20 seconds on each side. While they are warm, use a small knife to slice open an edge on each gordita, slicing about half the gordita open. Fill the pocket with 2 tablespoons of Drunken Beans, 2 tablespoons of the potato mixture, and a light garnish of cilantro or epazote.

Make It Low-Fat: Instead of frying the gorditas, cook the gorditas for 2 1/2 minutes per side over medium heat on a griddle, cut them open as soon as they come off the griddle, and then stuff them.

Mushroom and Tomatillo Salsa Chalupas
Chalupas de Hongos y Salsa Verde

MAKE 8 CHALUPAS

Chalupas come in several shapes and sizes. In some regions of Mexico, they are oblong "boats" (in fact, the word "chalupa" refers to a canoe), and in other places, they are simply tortillas fried in a shallow bowl shape, while in Puebla, their famous chalupas are merely the size of a silver dollar. Whatever the case, they are always a thin indented corn "tortilla" filled with some of the most delicious food I've ever had. The version I prefer is the canoe-shaped version, found below, but if you want to make the silver dollar–size ones, I've provided instructions on how to make those.

Chalupas:
1 1/2 cups Homemade Masa (page 23)

Filling:
1 tablespoon olive oil
16 to 20 cremini mushrooms, lightly rinsed, patted dry, and quartered
6 cloves garlic, minced
1 tablespoon minced fresh epazote, optional
1/4 teaspoon salt
1 cup Salsa Verde (page 50)
2 ripe Hass avocados, pitted, peeled, and coarsely chopped

Chalupas: Divide the masa into 8 portions and roll them into cigar shapes about 3 1/2 inches long and 1/2 inch in diameter. Line each plate of a tortilla press with plastic wrap, place one of the pieces of masa in the center, and press it into an oval shape. Repeat until you have pressed all the masa. Keep the ovals covered with a slightly damp towel or piece of plastic wrap so they don't dry out.

Heat a comal or griddle over medium heat. Place an oval on the comal or griddle and toast it for 2 minutes. Flip the oval and toast it for 1 more minute. As it toasts, use your fingers to gently curl the sides of the oval up to form a 1/4-inch rim. Be careful, and if you are not comfortable doing this directly on the griddle, transfer the chalupa to a plate, curl the rim, then return it to the comal or griddle. Make sure you curl the cooked side up. Repeat this process until you have cooked all the chalupas.

Filling: Heat the oil in a medium skillet over medium-high heat. Add the creminis and cook them until they are lightly browned, about 5 minutes. Add the garlic, epazote, and salt and cook 1 more minute. Set the mushroom mixture aside. To serve, top each chalupa with 2 tablespoons Salsa Verde, 2 tablespoons of the filling, and a few pieces of chopped avocado.

Huaraches with Cactus, Beans, Guajillo Sauce, and Crema

Huaraches de Nopales, Frijoles, Salsa Guajillo y Crema

MAKES 4 HUARACHES

Whenever I think of huaraches, I am reminded of the smells of toasted corn and cooked beans from the street stalls of Mexico. They are rustic and intoxicating and happen to be fairly easy to duplicate at home. Like many other antojitos, a myriad of toppings can be used on them, but the heart of the huarache is that oblong-shaped corn dough, wrapped around a filling of beans and toasted on a hot comal.

Huaraches:
1 1/4 cups Drunken Beans (page 30) or beans of your choice
1 1/2 cups Homemade Masa (page 23), divided into 4 portions

Toppings:
1 tablespoon corn or olive oil
2 cactus paddles, trimmed and cut into 2 x 3/4-inch strips
1/2 teaspoon salt
1 cup Basic Guajillo Chile Sauce (page 43) or Crushed Red Salsa (page 48)
1/2 cup vegan sour cream, stirred vigorously

Huaraches: Heat a comal or medium skillet over medium heat. Purée the Drunken Beans in a blender or food processor and set them aside. Roll each portion of the masa into an oval-shaped ball. Using your thumb, press a large indentation, one that can handle 3 tablespoons of filling, into each of the balls. Fill each indentation with 2 to 3 tablespoons of beans. Pinch the dough up around the beans to completely close the huaraches and gently roll them into a thick cigar shape about 4 1/2 to 5 inches long. Line a tortilla press with plastic wrap. Place a huarache in the press and gently press it closed until it's about 1/3-inch thick. Repeat this process with the other huaraches. Transfer them to the hot comal or griddle and cook them for 1 minute, then flip and cook them for 2 more minutes.

Toppings: Heat the oil in a medium skillet over high heat and sauté the cactus strips with the salt until the strips are lightly browned, about 6 to 7 minutes.

To serve, drizzle 1/4 cup of the Basic Guajillo Chile Sauce or Crushed Red Salsa over each huarache, then top with the cactus strips, and drizzle 2 tablespoons of the sour cream over each.

Make It Simple: Use canned refried black beans instead of making your own, use your favorite red salsa instead of making guajillo sauce.

Other Topping Ideas:

- Chopped lettuce, minced fresh tomatoes, and minced serrano chiles
- Battered and fried squash blossoms and roasted garlic
- Guacamole and minced chipotles in adobo

Sope

Gordita

Chalupa

Huarache

Quesadillas Two Ways
Quesadillas de Flor de Calabaza y Quesadillas de Frijoles Negros

MAKES 8 (5-INCH) OR 4 (7-INCH) QUESADILLAS

The key to quesadillas is getting the cheese melted without overcooking the tortilla. You'll want to keep the heat a bit low to do that. In Northern Mexico and north of the border, quesadillas are often made with flour tortillas, but in the rest of Mexico, it's corn all the way. The best ones are made with fresh, uncooked corn tortillas, but for simplicity, you can use store-bought. You'll also want to choose a good vegan cheese for this recipe. I often make my own vegan cheeses, but if I'm using a packaged one, I typically shred up some Teese Vegan Mozzarella Cheese, as it's the closest to a white melting Mexican cheese.

Squash Blossom Quesadilla Filling:
8 squash blossoms
3 tablespoons minced fresh epazote, optional
3 poblano chiles, roasted, peeled, seeded, and cut into 1/2-inch thick
    strips
1 1/2 cups shredded vegan white cheese

Black Bean Quesadilla Filling:
1 cup cooked black beans, rinsed
4 chipotles in adobo, chopped
1 1/2 cups shredded vegan white cheese

Tortillas (choose one of the following):
8 (5-inch) uncooked corn tortillas (page 25)
8 (5-inch) store-bought corn tortillas (see below for instructions to make
    quesadillas using store-bought corn tortillas)
4 (7-inch) flour tortillas (page 26)

Squash Blossom filling: In a bowl, combine the squash blossoms, epazote (if using), chiles, and vegan cheese. Mix well.

Black Bean filling: In a bowl, combine the black beans, chipotles, and vegan cheese. Mix well.

Divide the squash blossom filling or the black bean chipotle filling equally among all the tortillas. In all cases, heat a medium skillet to just below medium heat and have its lid within reach. The method for making quesadillas with uncooked corn tortillas and flour tortillas is the same.

Uncooked Corn Tortillas and Flour Tortillas: Place some of the quesadilla filling on one side of an uncooked corn tortilla, leaving at least a 3/4-inch space from the edge. Fold the tortilla over and lightly pinch it closed. Repeat this process until you have enough quesadillas to fill your pan. Place the quesadillas in the pan and cover it with its lid. After 2 minutes, gently flip the quesadillas, cover the pan again, and cook 2 more minutes.

Store-Bought Corn Tortillas: Instead of only spreading the filling on one side, spread the filling all across the tortilla, leaving a 3/4-inch rim around the edge. Do not fold the tortillas yet. Lay them in the pan, cover it with a lid, and cook the quesadillas 2 minutes. Fold the tortilla in half and serve. These don't require as much time as the other style since the heat is being applied to the entire tortillas and filling the whole time.

Other Filling Ideas:

- 1/3 cup chopped huitlacoche, 1/2 teaspoon freshly cracked black pepper, and 1 1/2 cups shredded vegan white cheese
- 1 cup chard, wilted in Garlic-Citrus Olive Oil (page 43); 1/2 cup Roasted Chile Strips (page 39); and 1 1/2 cups shredded vegan white cheese

Tostadas with Hearts of Palm Ceviche
Tostadas de Ceviche

MAKES 8 TOSTADAS

A Baja favorite, and one of mine as well, these tostadas aren't your usual bean-and-cheese affair. These are lively and fun, zesty and spicy, light and crispy. I usually eat two or three of these at a sitting, and I always make a double batch of the filling, which only gets better as it ages. That way, I can have them again the next day in just a few minutes. Feel free to use a good-quality, store-bought tostada, but for the absolute freshest flavor, make your own. I also use tofu as an option to make these heartier as a meal. The diced baked tofu is perfect for these crispy treats, and combined with the hearts of palm, lend a real seafood-like quality.

8 (3-inch) hearts of palm pieces, fresh or jarred, but not canned
3 Roma tomatoes, seeded and coarsely chopped into 1/4-inch pieces
2 serrano chiles, seeded and minced
1/2 small red onion, minced
2 ripe Hass avocados, pitted, peeled, and chopped
1/2 cup chopped fresh cilantro
1/2 teaspoon dried Mexican oregano
1/2 teaspoon coarse sea salt

1/2 cup fresh lime juice

3 tablespoons olive oil

1 (8-ounce) package savory baked tofu, cut into 1/4-inch dice, optional

8 (5-inch) Basic Corn Tortillas (page 25) or store-bought corn tortillas

Corn oil, for frying

Chipotle chile flakes, optional, for garnishing

Smash the hearts of palm a few times using a molcajete (mortar and pestle) or in a mixing bowl with a potato masher. In a medium bowl, combine the hearts of palm, tomatoes, serranos, onion, avocados, cilantro, Mexican oregano, salt, lime juice, olive oil, and tofu (if using). Let this sit for at least an hour. If it is going to sit for more than 2 hours, cover it with plastic wrap and keep it refrigerated. It will last about a day refrigerated.

Add about 1/2 inch of corn oil to a medium pan and heat it to 375°F, until it's hot but not smoking. Fry a tortilla on both sides for about 1 minute, until crispy, then it set aside on a paper towel to cool and drain. Top each fried tortilla with about 1/4 to 1/3 cup of the hearts of palm mixture. Garnish with the crushed chipotle chile flakes if you want it spicier.

Make It Without Oil: Omit the olive oil from the ceviche. Bake the tortillas in the oven at 250°F for 10 minutes, until crunchy.

Jicama-on-a-Stick
with Lime and Pequín Chile Powder
Jicaleta

MAKES 4 TO 6 JICALETAS

This is one of my favorite quick summer treats. It's refreshing, spicy, tart, and easy to make. Just slice jicama into popsicle (*paleta* in Spanish) shapes, insert a popsicle stick, and dress the jicama with chile and lime.

1 medium jicama, peeled and cut into popsicle shapes about 1/2-inch thick

Juice of 4 limes

1/4 cup pequín chile powder

Insert a popsicle stick into each slice of jicama. Dress the jicama with lime juice and sprinkle pequín chile powder onto the jicama until well coated.

Salted Lime Plantain Tacos, page 83

TACOS

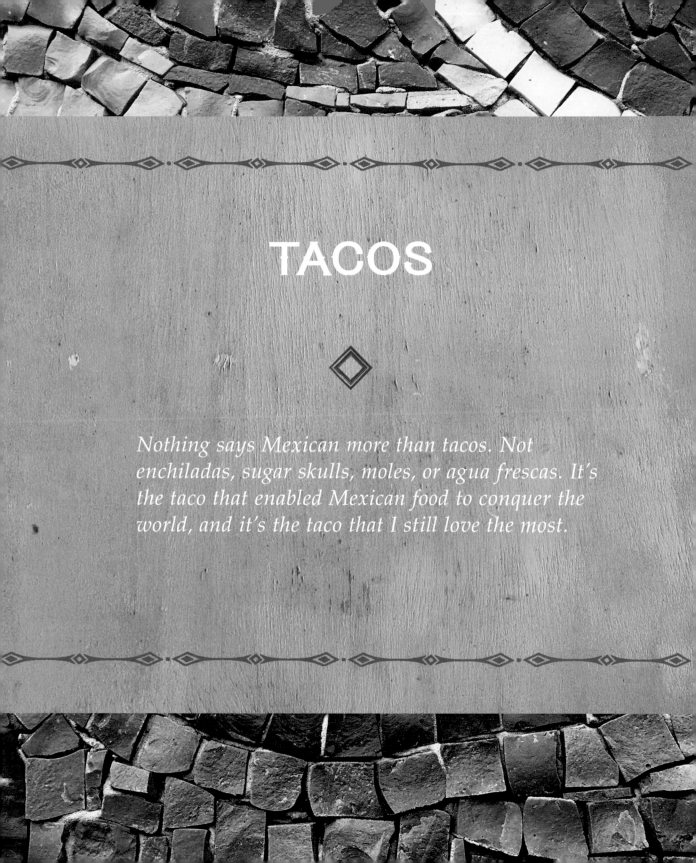

Nothing says Mexican more than tacos. Not enchiladas, sugar skulls, moles, or agua frescas. It's the taco that enabled Mexican food to conquer the world, and it's the taco that I still love the most.

Real Mexican tacos are lively, balanced with contrasting flavors and textures, and all held together in a soulful tortilla. In fact, many taco aficionados, myself included, hold that the tortilla is the heart of the taco. A good tortilla will uplift an average taco and a bad tortilla will drag down what would otherwise be a great one. That's why I almost always make my own tortillas when I make tacos. Of course, if you're in a rush, feel free to use store-bought tortillas. Just make sure to warm them up, either by steaming them for about 15 seconds, or warming them over medium heat in a dry pan for about 10 seconds per side. If you don't warm them, they tend to crack and you end up with a messy taco salad. Also, nearly all authentic tacos are served with corn tortillas, though not exclusively. Flour tortillas are also used in Northern Mexico, especially in the border towns. In fact, a few of the recipes in this chapter use flour tortillas.

Speaking of tortillas, true taco-size tortillas are typically much smaller than other tortillas, even the ones sold in supermarkets designated for tacos. Most authentic corn tortillas are about four inches in diameter and tacos are served two and three at a time. There's a very good chance your local Mexican market will have these for sale, but if you don't want to make a special trip for them and you don't want to make your own, use what you can find. Just keep in mind that most of the recipe yields in this chapter are for the authentic street taco-size tortillas. You'll want to adjust accordingly. If you are going to use store-bought tortillas, I recommend the white handmade tortillas from Trader Joe's. They have a good flavor and are thick enough that they don't easily fall apart once they are properly warmed.

So what makes a taco so special? The answer is that it's not just one thing. It's the warm, inviting flavor of a fresh tortilla; it's the flavors that sizzle and jump on the palate; it's the fun of eating a handheld food; it's the balance of all the components, from the tortilla to the filling to the condiments to the salsa; and most importantly, it's a food that makes people smile. If you're looking for more authentic taco recipes, check out my book *Vegan Tacos: Authentic and Inspired Recipes for Mexico's Favorite Street Food* published by Vegan Heritage Press. You will never look at tacos the same way.

Salted Lime Plantain Tacos
Tacos de Plátanos de Limon y Sal

MAKES 12 TACOS

These tacos are my own creation. Whenever I see semi-ripe plantains at the store, I buy a few so I can make these treasures. The key is to make sure the plantains have a few black splotches on the skin. That's an indication that they're just a little bit sweet, but still starchy and hearty enough to stand up to the grill, although if you don't want to grill them, you can easily make them in a sauté pan. Regardless of how they're cooked, I love the different flavor contrasts with these tacos. Soulful corn tortillas, sweet plantains, crunchy pepitas and cabbage, bright lime, and crema to tie everything together.

> **2 medium semi-ripe plantains, peeled and sliced in half lengthwise**
> **1 tablespoon Garlic-Citrus Olive Oil (page 43), garlic-infused oil, or olive oil**
> **1 teaspoon coarse salt**
> **Zest of 2 limes**
> **Juice of 2 limes**
> **12 (4-inch) corn tortillas**
> **1 cup shredded purple cabbage**
> **1/4 cup salted roasted pepitas**
> **Salsa Verde (page 50)**
> **Vegan sour cream, whipped vigorously**

Light your grill and let the coals turn white or bring a gas grill to medium-high heat. Toss the plantain halves in the Garlic-Citrus Olive Oil and grill them on both sides until char lines appear. Remove the plantains from the grill, chop them into 1-inch pieces, and immediately toss them with the salt, lime zest, and lime juice. Warm the tortillas, add the grilled plantains to them, and top with shredded cabbage, pepitas, Salsa Verde, and sour cream.

Note: You can make these in a large skillet by bringing the Garlic-Citrus Olive Oil to medium-high heat and sautéing the plantains until lightly browned. Remove them from the pan and immediately toss with the salt, lime zest, and lime juice.

Gringa Tacos
Tacos Gringas

MAKES 4 TACOS

One of those rare tacos made with wheat flour tortillas, these supposedly get their name from the freckled look the flour tortillas acquire when placed on the griddle and the use of ingredients more commonly found north of the border, like the melted cheese and, of course, the flour tortillas. Nomenclature aside, these tacos are crazy delicious, taking the best parts of tacos al pastor and quesadillas and fusing them together. Because the filling for tacos al pastor takes a while to make and is more properly done on a spit, I made these with an easy cheat you can do in a sauté pan. You can find adodo sauce and achiote paste at a Mexican market.

1 tablespoon corn or olive oil
1 1/2 cups diced fresh or canned pineapple
1 large eggplant, cut into 1 x 4-inch strips, or 2 1/2 cups meatless strips
1/2 teaspoon salt
1/4 cup adobo sauce from 1 (7-ounce) can chipotles in adobo
1 tablespoon achiote paste (also known as recado rojo)
1 cup shredded vegan white cheese
8 (5- to 6-inch) flour tortillas (page 26)
1/4 cup minced fresh cilantro
1 small white onion, minced
1 lime, cut into 4 wedges, for serving
Salsa of your choice, for serving

Heat the oil in a large skillet over medium-high heat. Add the pineapple (be careful of splattering oil) and sear it until it is browned. Remove it from the skillet and set it aside. Add the eggplant or meatless strips and salt and cook for 5 to 6 minutes, stirring occasionally. Turn the heat down to medium. Add the adobo sauce and achiote paste and cook for 2 more minutes, then remove the skillet from the heat.

While the eggplant mixture is cooking, heat a griddle over medium heat. Spread the vegan cheese on top of 4 of the tortillas, then lay the other 4 tortillas on top of the cheese. You should have four stacks that are comprised of two tortillas each with vegan cheese sandwiched between. Place these on the griddle and place a lid over them to help the cheese melt. Once the cheese is melted, remove the tortillas from the griddle and place the eggplant mixture and pineapple on top of the tortilla stacks right down the middle, just like a taco. Garnish with the cilantro and onion, then fold the tortillas up to make the Tacos Gringas. Serve with lime wedges and salsa.

Make It Simple: If you can't find adobo sauce and achiote paste, skip those ingredients and dress the eggplant or meatless strips with 1 tablespoon of the chile powder of your choice immediately after the filling comes off the heat for a pared down, easier version of this recipe.

Tacos with Beans, Greens, and Red Chile Sauce

Tacos de Frijoles y Alcega en Salsa Roja

MAKES 8 TACOS

These tacos are incredibly easy to make and so delicious, you won't even think about how healthy they are. Feel free to dress them up however you like, whether that's adding in crunchy purple cabbage, fried chiles de árbol, pepitas, Simple Queso Fresco (page 42), or Pickled Onions (page 39). When I make these, though, I'm looking for something hearty, tasty, and simple, so I rarely bother with any condiments. My only indulgence is that I make the tortillas myself.

1 large bunch chard, leaves sliced into ribbons and stems sliced paper thin

1 1/2 cups cooked pinto beans, rinsed

Pinch salt

1/2 batch Basic Guajillo Chile Sauce (page 43)

8 (5-inch) Basic Corn Tortillas (page 25) or store-bought corn tortillas

Optional Garnishes:
Sliced radish
Sliced purple cabbage
Fried chiles de árbol
Pepitas
Simple Queso Fresco (page 42) or other crumbly vegan cheese
Pickled Onions (page 39)

Simmer the chard, beans, and salt in the sauce in a medium saucepan over medium heat until the chard wilts and the sauce thickens around the beans and greens. Warm the tortillas and serve immediately. Serve with as many optional garnishes as you like.

Battleship Tacos
Tacos Acorazados

MAKES 4 TACOS

These tacos originated in Cuernavaca, Morelos, but they're so good, you can find them from the streets of Mexico City to the taco trucks of Los Angeles. They are called battleship tacos because they're so big that they need two full-size corn tortillas to hold all the fillings. And oh, those fillings! Red rice, crispy milanesa, jalapeño rajas, onion, and some optional toppings like cactus, beans, and fried potatoes. You may want to go at these tacos with a fork. I provide two ways to make the milanesa (breaded and fried zucchinis or meatless cutlets), so choose the one that makes you happy.

Corn oil
1 small white onion, cut into 1/4-inch wide strips
1/2 cup unbleached all-purpose flour
3/4 teaspoon salt
1/2 teaspoon freshly ground black pepper
1/2 cup water or beer
1/2 cup dry bread crumbs
2 large zucchini, cut into 2-inch long, 3/4-inch thick pieces or 4 small meatless cutlets
8 (5- to 6-inch) corn tortillas
2 cups Mexican Red Rice (page 34), made without the carrots and peas
4 jalapeños, roasted, seeded, and cut in half

Optional Toppings:
Chopped ripe Hass avocado
Pinto beans
Fried potatoes
Sautéed cactus strips
Fresh tomato
Simple Queso Fresco (page 42)

Add about 1/4 inch of corn oil to a large skillet and heat the oil over medium-high heat. Add the onion strips and sauté them for 2 minutes, then remove them from the skillet and set them aside.

To make the milanesa, combine the flour, salt, pepper, and water or beer in a medium bowl. Put the bread crumbs in a separate bowl. Dunk the zucchini strips or cutlets in the flour mixture, then dredge them through the bread crumbs. Gently arrange them in the skillet and fry them until the bread crumbs turn golden brown, about 4 minutes per side. Remove them from the skillet and transfer them to a paper towel. If you are using the cutlets, slice them into 1-inch strips once they cool.

Warm the tortillas and make 4 stacks of 2 tortillas each. Top each stack with about 1/2 cup of the Mexican Red Rice, the milanesa, jalapeños, and any optional toppings you like, then fold the stacks up to make giant tacos. I'm a particular fan of cactus and avocado for this taco.

Time-Saving Tip: Start cooking the rice before you do anything else for this recipe.

Pirate Tacos
Tacos Piratas

MAKES 4 TACOS

Tacos have cool names. Battleship Tacos. Pirate Tacos. The only thing cooler would be Ninja tacos, and they probably exist somewhere. These tacos are from Monterrey and proudly show their northern heritage, much like their sister taco, the Taco Gringa (my version of which you can find on page 84), fashioned from flour tortillas and melted cheese. They're most commonly served after hours, intended to quell the late-night munchies after a night of bar hopping and cervezas.

1 tablespoon corn or olive oil

2 large portobello mushrooms, lightly rinsed, patted dry, and chopped into 1-inch pieces, or 2 cups meatless strips

1 poblano chile, finely chopped

1/2 teaspoon salt

1/2 teaspoon freshly ground black pepper

3/4 cup shredded vegan white cheese

4 (5- to 6-inch) flour tortillas, brushed with corn or olive oil on one side

1 ripe Hass avocado, pitted, peeled, and coarsely chopped

1 small white onion, minced

1/4 cup finely chopped fresh cilantro

1 lime, cut into 4 wedges, for serving

Salsa of your choice, for serving

Heat a large skillet at just above medium heat, then add the oil. Add the mushrooms (or meatless strips) poblano, salt, and pepper and cook for 5 to 6 minutes, stirring occasionally.

While the mushroom mixture is cooking, heat a griddle over medium heat. Spread the vegan cheese on each tortilla on the unbrushed side, then divide the mushroom filling among the 4 tortillas. Add the avocado, onion, and cilantro and fold the tortillas in half. Lay them on the griddle and cook them until browned, usually 2 to 3 minutes. Flip the tortillas and repeat. Serve with the lime wedges and salsa.

Bean and Cheese Sandwiches with Pico de Gallo, page 99

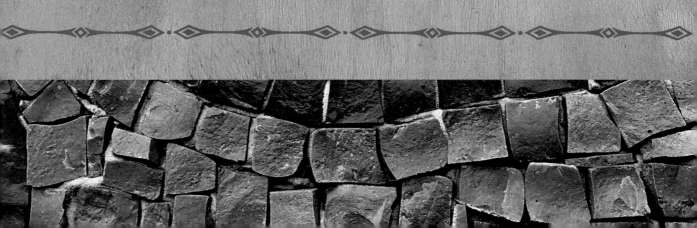

TORTAS AND OTHER SANDWICHES

Tortas, Pambazos, Cemitas y Mas

Mexican sandwiches are to the world of sandwiches what metal is to the world of music. They are in-your-face extravaganzas of heat and flavors and one of the most addicting foods you can eat.

T ry eating a torta smothered in chile de árbol salsa and then go back and eat that plain old sandwich of Tofurky slices and vegan mayo. If you're like me, you just can't do it. If you can, let me tempt you with a torta.

Tortas are the most commonly known Mexican sandwiches. They're usually served on telera bread, a three-humped soft roll, but you can also find them served on bolillo rolls and the famous torta ahogada is served on a roll called birote salado. They often come with sliced cabbage and radish, plenty of hot sauce choices, onions, and pickled jalapeños. When you order a torta, you'll have a choice of condiments, but let me suggest getting your sandwich con todo (i.e., "with everything"). This is the way it was meant to be served, and you won't be disappointed, though your tongue may be on fire.

Ironically, tortas didn't used to be such extravagant affairs. Up until the 1960s, nearly every torta was served cold and only featured a few simple ingredients. Then came the hot tortas de fuegos, and the street was taken over by these hot Mexican sandwiches. You could say the old-style tortas were left out in the cold. Tortas and other sandwiches are typically afternoon meals and, unlike tacos, tortas are hard to find before noon. They can be complex or simple sandwiches, but they are always in-your-face full of flavor and usually pretty messy. So, grab a lot of napkins, an agua fresca, and a friend, and get to making some tortas.

There are, of course, sandwiches that are not tortas, like the pambazo and cemita, but they serve the same purpose as the torta. Their different names come from the bread with which they are made. I've noticed more and more that "torta" is simply becoming the general term for "sandwich."

My local Mexican market makes all the different types of bread for these sandwiches, but that hasn't always been the case, and you may not have access to the same breads. If so, you can make your own breads using the baking recipes in this book, or you can substitute vegan kaiser rolls or ciabatta rolls for the telera bread and French baguettes for the bolillo rolls. You'll still have an incredible sandwich.

Create Your Own Torta

So you want to create your own torta recipe. I don't blame you. Tortas are fun and easy to make. Here are a few guidelines to making your own torta masterpiece. Not all tortas follow these guidelines to the letter, but a lot of them do:

- Choose a telera or bolillo roll (or one of their substitutes) and lightly toast it.
- Spread mashed or puréed beans on the bottom of the bread.
- Add a filling, which can be more beans, grilled veggies, vegan carnitas, or anything that will make a substantial sandwich.
- Add something creamy, such as avocado.
- Serve with a salsa or add it directly to the torta.
- Serve with pickled jalapeños, shredded cabbage, sliced radish, and lime wedges.

Fried Shredded Seitan Sandwich
Pelona

MAKES 2 SANDWICHES

The cemita may be the preferred sandwich of Puebla, but the pelona, a fried sandwich loaded with avocado and other goodies, is its simple, more manageable cousin. The key is getting the bread nice and crispy. It should feel like it's falling apart in your mouth and if it crumbles in the hand a bit, that's OK, because there's a healthy serving of crema oozing out the side to catch those golden crumbs. I never promised it wouldn't be messy, and it's well worth the extra napkins.

- **Corn or safflower oil, for frying**
- **1 cup shredded seitan**
- **1/2 cup dried mushrooms (any kind)**
- **1/2 teaspoon freshly ground black pepper**
- **Salt, to taste**
- **2 pelona rolls or round sandwich rolls, such as vegan kaiser rolls, sliced in half**
- **1 ripe Hass avocado, pitted, peeled, and coarsely chopped**
- **1/2 cup shredded lettuce**
- **1/3 cup vegan sour cream, whipped vigorously**
- **Hot sauce, to taste**

Add a 1/8-inch layer of oil to a large cast iron pot (or other pot big enough to fry the bread) over medium heat. Add the shredded seitan, mushrooms, pepper, and salt and sauté for about 5 minutes. Remove the seitan mixture from the pot and set aside. Add enough oil to the pot to cover the sandwich rolls and bring it to 375°F. Add the sandwich rolls (working in batches, if necessary) and fry the bread until it is golden and crispy. The time will vary based on the type of bread used, but expect 3 to 5 minutes.

On the bottom rolls, layer the avocado, lettuce, the seitan mixture, sour cream, and hot sauce. Close the sandwiches with the top buns and serve immediately.

Baked Version: Instead of frying the rolls, bake them at 450°F for 5 to 6 minutes, until crispy but not hard.

Bean and Avocado Sandwich Drowned in Salsa

Torta Ahogada

MAKES 2 TORTAS

This is my favorite torta. It's easy to make and one of the spiciest meals you'll ever eat. It's a sandwich stuffed with beans and avocado and swimming in a killer spicy chile de árbol sauce. You can tone down that sauce by adding tomatoes to it, but its true incarnation, made from just chiles de árbol, vinegar, and spices, is called muerta. That's right. It's so spicy, it's called "death sauce." I love it. The torta is the signature sandwich of Guadalajara and it was supposedly created when, in the early 1900s, a street vendor named De La Torre accidentally dropped a sandwich into a vat of salsa. The customer who was supposed to get the sandwich cried out, "You drowned it!" He ate it anyway and loved it, and the torta ahogada was born. Traditionally, these are made from birrote salado, a crusty salted bread, but a bolillo roll or crusty baguette will do in a pinch.

Tortas:
2 birrote or bolillo rolls or 6-inch long baguettes split in half about 3/4 of the way through the bread
1 cup Refried Beans (page 30) using black beans or store-bought refried black beans
1 ripe Hass avocado, pitted, peeled, and cut into 1/4-inch thick slices

Sauce:
30 chiles de árbol, stemmed, seeded, and rehydrated
3 cloves garlic
3/4 cup white vinegar (white balsamic works best)
1 cup water
1 teaspoon dried Mexican oregano
1/2 teaspoon ground cumin
1/2 teaspoon freshly ground black pepper
1/8 teaspoon ground cloves
1 teaspoon salt

Garnishes:
2 radishes, thinly sliced
8 to 12 white Pickled Onions (page 39), separated into rings, or raw white onion rings
Lime wedges

Tortas: Lightly toast the rolls or baguettes. Warm the beans and spread them evenly in each roll. Add the avocado slices. Place the sandwiches in bowls.

Sauce: In a blender or food processor, purée the chiles de árbol, garlic, vinegar, water, Mexican oregano, cumin, pepper, cloves, and salt. (Strain it if you want a very smooth sauce.) Pour the sauce over the sandwiches. Garnish the sandwiches with the sliced radishes and Pickled Onions and serve with the lime wedges. Eat these tortas with a fork or lots of napkins.

Less Spicy Option: Omit the water and add 1 to 3 cups crushed fire-roasted tomatoes and omit or decrease the chiles de árbol, to your taste.

Portobello Sandwich
Pepito de Hongo

This steak sandwich is a hallmark of Mexico City torterias. I make mine with a thick portobello mushroom instead of steak, though I'm not above using a thick piece of seitan when I want something incredibly hearty. I also like using whole chipotles in adobo, instead of the more traditional pickled jalapeños. I am an admitted glutton for spicy food.

- 1 tablespoon olive oil
- 1 large portobello mushroom cap
- 1 teaspoon vegan Worcestershire sauce
- Juice of 1/2 lime
- 1/8 teaspoon salt
- 1/4 teaspoon coarsely ground black pepper
- 1 tablespoon vegan butter or olive oil
- 1 6-inch-long baguette, halved lengthwise
- 3 tablespoons refried black beans
- Pickled jalapeños, to taste
- Vegan mayonnaise, to taste
- Dijon mustard, to taste
- 3 tablespoons Salsa Verde (page 50), optional
- 3 to 4 ripe Hass avocado slices
- 3 to 4 white onion rings, about 1/4-inch thick

Heat the oil in a small skillet over medium-high heat. Add the portobello mushroom cap and sauté on both sides until it is barely softened, about 3 minutes on the first side and 1 minute on the second side. Reduce the heat to medium and add the Worcestershire sauce, lime juice, salt, and pepper and quickly flip the mushroom until the sauce cooks onto it. Remove it from the skillet and set it aside.

Add the butter to the skillet. Once it melts, place the baguette, cut-side down, in the skillet and toast it for 3 minutes. Remove it from the skillet.

Spread the beans and jalapeños on the bottom half of the baguette. Spread the mayonnaise and mustard on the top half. Add the portobello, Salsa Verde (if using), avocado slices, and onion rings, close, and eat!

Bean and Cheese Sandwich with Pico de Gallo

Mollete

MAKES 2 SANDWICHES

Molletes (pronounced "moh-YAY-tays") are classic bean and cheese sandwiches. This is my quick, go-to Mexican comfort food, because it only takes a few minutes to put together and it's homey and satisfying. Pico de gallo is the usual salsa served with this sandwich, but I'll use pickled jalapeños, minced serrano chiles, pickled habaneros, or a chipotle salsa just as readily. (See photo on page 92.)

1 bolillo roll or 6-inch-long baguette, halved lengthwise

1 to 2 tablespoons melted vegan butter or olive oil

1/2 cup refried black beans

1/3 cup finely chopped vegan provolone or shredded vegan white cheese

1/2 cup Pico de Gallo (page 47)

Ripe Hass avocado slices, optional

Preheat an oven or toaster oven to 500°F. Brush the cut side of the bread with the butter or olive oil. In a large skillet over medium heat, toast the bread cut-side down for 2 minutes. Spread 1/4 cup of refried black beans on each piece of bread, then cover the beans with the cheese. Bake for 3 to 5 minutes, just until the cheese has started to melt. Top with Pico de Gallo and avocado slices (if using). Serve immediately.

Potato and Chorizo Sandwich
Pambazo

Like many sandwiches, pambazos steal their name from the name of the bread on which they're served. The name is derived from pan basso, a lower-quality bread made from inferior flour that was common during the late 1800s in Mexico. The most common version of this sandwich is stuffed with potatoes and chorizo, dipped into a guajillo chile sauce, and fried crisp. Small versions of these sandwiches, called pambacitos, are often served at parties.

- 2 tablespoons corn oil, plus more for frying
- 4 medium Yukon gold potatoes, cut into 1/2-inch pieces
- 3/4 teaspoon salt
- 3/4 cup Red Chorizo (page 40) or store-bought vegan chorizo
- 4 vegan pambazo, vegan kaiser, or bolillo rolls (see note)
- 4 cups Basic Guajillo Chile Sauce (page 43)
- 1 cup shredded lettuce
- 1/2 cup vegan sour cream, whipped vigorously
- 1 cup Simple Queso Fresco (page 42) or 1/2 cup chopped salted roasted
  peanuts

Heat the oil in a large skillet over medium heat. Add the potatoes and salt and cook, stirring occasionally, until the potatoes are slightly browned, about 10 minutes. Add the Red Chorizo, stir, and cook 1 minute Distribute the potato-chorizo mixture among the rolls and close them, pressing them tight. Add 1/2 inch corn oil to the skillet and bring it to medium-high heat.

Quickly dip a sandwich in the Basic Guajillo Chile Sauce and transfer the sandwich to the skillet. Be careful, because the oil will spatter. Fry the bottom of the bun until it is crisp, flip the sandwich, and fry the top. Repeat this process with the other sandwiches.

Open up the sandwiches and garnish them with shredded lettuce, sour cream, Simple Queso Fresco or peanuts, and a couple spoonfuls of leftover chile sauce. Close and serve.

Note: The pambazo roll is ideal, because it can hold up after being drenched in the sauce, but you can use semi-stale bread or rolls to get the same effect.

Make It in the Oven: Instead of frying the sandwich, preheat the oven to 500°F and bake the sandwiches for 10 minutes instead of frying them.

Black Bean and Poblano Chile Torta
Torta de Frijoles Negro y Rajas

MAKES 2 SANDWICHES

This torta is one of my own creations and, although it has a long ingredient list, it comes together without a lot of hassle. It's basically a bean and chile sandwich with a garlicky vegan mayo spread. I often make extra filling and aioli just so I can have another sandwich the next day.

Filling and Toppings:
1 poblano chile
2 1/2 cups meatless strips or 3 cups chopped oyster mushrooms or 2 cups
   quartered cremini mushrooms
1/2 cup water
4 cloves garlic, minced
3 tablespoons guajillo chile powder
3/4 teaspoon dried Mexican oregano
1/4 teaspoon salt
2 tablespoons white balsamic vinegar or distilled white vinegar
3/4 cup refried black beans
1/2 cup shredded vegan cheese, optional

Roasted Garlic Aioli:
10 cloves roasted garlic (see page 18)
1/2 cup vegan mayonnaise
Juice of 2 limes
1/4 teaspoon salt
Indian black salt, optional, for garnishing

Bread:
2 bolillo or telera rolls, halved (see note)

Pan-roast the poblano, seed it, cut it into 1/2-inch thick strips, and set aside. While the poblano is pan-roasting, make the aioli. Purée the garlic, mayonnaise, lime juice, and salt in a blender or food processor and set aside.

In a small pot over medium heat, simmer the meatless strips or mushrooms in the water, garlic, chile powder, oregano, salt, and vinegar for 10 minutes. If you need to add a splash of water to keep the sauce hydrated, do so. Ultimately, the sauce should cook down so it coats the filling.

Pull out a small amount of bread from the center of each half of the rolls, creating shallow boats in which the filling and toppings can sit. Toast the bread in a toaster, in the oven, or in a buttered skillet. Spread the filling on the bottom halves of bread and top with the poblano strips. Spread the black beans and then the aioli on the top portions of bread and sprinkle it with the Indian black salt. (Don't close the sandwich, because the Indian black salt makes a nice presentation.)

For a more decadent version of this sandwich, sprinkle the cheese on top of the filling and toast the bottom part of the sandwich until the cheese melts.

Note: If you can't find bolillo or telera rolls, you can use ciabatta rolls or small baguettes instead.

Make It Low-fat and Low-Sodium: Skip the aioli or use light silken tofu instead of the vegan mayonnaise. Do not use the optional vegan cheese. If you do it this way, the meal is incredibly low-fat. You can also omit the salt from the entirety of the recipe, though you will need to check the bread's sodium content.

Enchiladas in Red Sauce, page 108

ENCHILADAS

Enchiladas will always hold a special place in my heart. They're the first Mexican dish my mom taught me how to make and she, in turn, learned how to make them from her mother.

Enchiladas were simple on the surface, just corn tortillas lightly fried in oil, rolled in chile sauce, and wrapped around cheese and olives. It was only after she showed me how to make them that I realized the oil had to be just the right temperature, that the tortillas couldn't linger in the chile sauce, and that there was a gentleness to folding them that kept the tortilla from tearing. It's not hard to make a good enchilada, but it takes a little practice to make a perfect one. Fortunately, practicing making enchiladas means getting to eat lots of enchiladas!

What is an enchilada, anyway? It's really just a corn tortilla enrobed in chile sauce. In fact, "enchilada" literally means "in chile sauce." If you take a tortilla and dredge it through a pan of chile sauce, you've got an enchilada. At some food stalls in Mexico, you'll find these simple chile-sauced tortillas lightly fried or griddled and served as quick snacks. At my house, I usually make them when I have leftover chile sauce from other dishes. I always have corn tortillas sitting around that I can dip in the sauce.

There are plenty of styles of enchiladas, but the three most common ones are flat, folded, and rolled.

Flat Enchiladas: These are most commonly referred to in the States as Sonoran-style enchiladas, even though they are found throughout Mexico and all over the American Southwest. In Mexico, flat enchiladas are often made with thick tortillas, almost like sopes, that are piled with toppings. In the Southwest, these are most frequently made with layers of thin tortillas and filling that looks more like lasagna, and then baked. Regardless of the region, flat enchiladas are a common way to serve them at home since they are so easy to make. Simply sauce a tortilla, lay it flat, top it with ingredients, bake if you like, and serve.

Folded Enchiladas: These are sauced tortillas filled with some sort of ingredient and folded over. Once they're folded, they are typically fried for a few seconds, and served topped with lettuce, crema, and sautéed veggies.

Rolled Enchiladas: These are the enchiladas you're probably used to seeing—tortillas in a chile sauce, rolled around a delicious filling. Frying the tortillas for about 3 seconds makes them pliable and keeps them from getting too wet from the chile sauce, which makes it easier to roll them and keep them rolled. Like other enchiladas, these can also be baked in the oven to finish them off. If you decide to bake them, make sure to coat your baking dish with some extra chile sauce so the enchiladas don't stick to the dish, and keep about a 1/2-inch gap between your enchiladas so they don't stick to each other.

Huastecas-Style Chorizo and Cactus Enchiladas

Enchiladas Huastecas

MAKES 12 ENCHILADAS

Enchiladas Huastecas are famous throughout the Potosina region. These delicious enchiladas are doused in a sweet and spicy tomato sauce and typically served alongside frijoles refritos and cecina. Cecina is a jerky marinated in sour orange juice. I make mine with cured eggplant, but neither the beans nor the eggplant cecina are necessary to enjoy enchiladas Huastecas. They're just a bonus.

Sauce:
6 Roma tomatoes
4 jalapeños, stemmed
1/4 cup water
2 tablespoons corn oil
1/2 medium white onion, cut into 1/4-inch dice
1/2 teaspoon salt
15 tepín chiles (wild pequín chiles) or chiles de árbol, toasted for 10 to 15 seconds, optional

Filling:
1 tablespoon corn or olive oil
1 1/2 cups cactus strips
1 cup Red Chorizo (page 40) or store-bought vegan chorizo
1/2 medium white onion, cut into 1/4-inch dice

Tortillas and Toppings:
12 (6-inch) corn tortillas
1/4 cup vegan sour cream, whipped vigorously
1/3 cup shredded vegan white cheese

Sauce: In a small pot, boil the tomatoes and jalapeños in the water until they are soft. Transfer the entire contents of the pot to a blender and purée. Set aside. In a deep skillet, heat the oil over medium heat. Add the onion and sauté until it is just browned. Add the reserved sauce, salt, and chiles, and cook for 7 to 8 minutes.

Filling: Heat the oil in a medium skillet over medium-high heat. Sauté the cactus strips until they are lightly browned, 8 to 10 minutes. Reduce the heat to medium, add the chorizo, stir, and cook for 3 to 4 minutes. Remove the cactus mixture from the heat, immediately add the onion, and stir to combine.

Warm the tortillas. Spoon 3 to 4 tablespoons of the sauce on each tortilla, then add 3 to 4 tablespoons of the filling to each tortilla and fold them over. Spoon another 2 to 3 tablespoons of sauce on top of each tortilla. Top each with 1 tablespoon of the vegan sour cream and a sprinkle of vegan cheese.

Enchiladas in Red Sauce
Enchiladas Rojas

MAKES 12 ENCHILADAS

Enchiladas rojas are common throughout Mexico. Not only are there plenty of regional styles, every family makes those styles differently. In Huasteca, some enchiladas rojas are made with chiles de árbol, while in Zacatecas, they're made primarily with ancho chiles. The fillings may change and the toppings may vary, but they are always done in a red chile sauce, commonly made with a combination of guajillo and ancho chiles. This version is one of my personal favorites, but you should feel free to fill them with your own favorite ingredients.

Filling:
3 large portobello mushrooms, lightly rinsed and patted dry
2 fresh ears corn, shucked
2 tablespoons olive oil
1/4 teaspoon coarse salt
3/4 cup refried black beans

Sauce:
4 guajillo chiles, stemmed, seeded, and rehydrated
4 ancho chiles, stemmed, seeded, and rehydrated
1 cup reserved chile water
Juice of 1 lime
1 teaspoon dried Mexican oregano
3/4 teaspoon salt

Tortillas:
Corn oil, for frying
12 (6-inch) corn tortillas

Toppings:
2 cups shredded red leaf lettuce
1/2 cup salted pepitas

Filling: If you have a wood-fire grill, light it with alder or mesquite wood, or use alder or mesquite chips soaked for an hour. If you have a gas grill, use soaked mesquite chips. Allow the flames to die down and the wood to get very hot. Brush the portobellos and corn with the olive oil and toss them in the salt. Grill them until the corn develops dark brown spots and the portobellos develop deep grill lines. On a very hot grill, this should take only about 5 minutes. Let the portobellos and corn cool until you can handle them, then slice the portobellos into 3/4-inch wide strips and cut the corn kernels off the cobs. Set aside.

Sauce: In a blender or food processor, purée the guajillos, anchos, chile water, lime juice, oregano, and salt. Heat the sauce in a medium skillet over low heat. Place a medium skillet on a burner next to the sauce and place a plate near the sauce. Add a 1/4-inch layer of oil to the skillet and bring it to 375°F. Add a tortilla to the oil for about 3 seconds.

Submerge the fried tortilla in the sauce for about 10 seconds, then transfer it to the plate. Slather 1 1/2 tablespoons of the refried black beans on one side of the tortilla and top the beans with about 3 portobello strips and 2 tablespoons of corn. Fold the tortilla in half and transfer to a plate. Repeat this process with the remaining tortillas.

Spread the remaining sauce evenly over the tortillas and top them with the shredded lettuce and pepitas.

Time-Saving Tip: Rehydrate the chiles for the sauce while you grill the portobellos and corn.

Note: If you don't have a grill, you can slice the portobellos and sauté them over high heat for 5 to 6 minutes in the oil and salt. Use the corn fresh instead of cooking it.

Enchiladas in Green Chile Sauce with Green Pipián

Enchiladas Verdes con Pipián Verde

MAKES 12 ENCHILADAS

Normally, enchiladas verdes are all about the roasted green chile sauce, but I wanted to add a decadent creamy component to these, so I top them with one of my favorite spreads, Pipián Verde, made from tomatillos and creamy pumpkin seeds. These two stars of the enchiladas go great together, but each can be used as individual components for other dishes. I often thin out the leftover chile sauce and use it as a soup base—I'll use Pipián Verde in anything.

Pipián Verde:
3 poblano chiles
2 jalapeños
1 1/2 cups water
3/4 teaspoon salt

Filling:
2 medium Mexican gray squash or zucchini, cut into 2 x 1/2-inch pieces
2 cups oyster mushroom pieces
2 tablespoons Garlic-Citrus Olive Oil (page 43) or olive oil
1/2 teaspoon salt
1/2 cup cooked hominy

Tortillas and Toppings:
Corn oil, for frying
12 (6-inch) corn tortillas
6 tomatillos, husked
1/2 cup salted roasted pepitas
2 cloves garlic
3 tablespoons white vinegar (preferably white balsamic)
1/2 teaspoon salt
3 dried chiles de árbol
1 teaspoon dried Mexican oregano
1/2 small white onion, cut into 1/8-inch thick rings

Preheat the oven to 450°F. In a medium baking dish, place the poblanos, jalapeños, and tomatillos. In another baking dish, toss the squash and oyster mushrooms with the Garlic-Citrus Olive Oil and salt. Bake both dishes for 30 minutes and remove them from the oven to cool.

Once the poblanos and jalapeños are cool enough to handle, peel, stem, and seed them. In a blender or food processor, purée the poblanos, jalapeños, water, and salt and transfer the sauce to a medium skillet. Keep the sauce warm over low heat.

Combine all the ingredients for the filling and set aside.

Add 1/4 inch of corn oil to a medium skillet and bring it to 375°F. Place a plate near the sauce. Fry a tortilla in the oil for 3 seconds, then submerge it in the chile sauce for about 10 seconds. Transfer the tortilla to the plate and add 3 tablespoons of the filling. Roll the tortilla closed, transfer it to a serving platter and repeat this process with the remaining tortillas. Pour the remaining sauce over the enchiladas.

In a food processor, purée the tomatillos, pepitas, garlic, vinegar, salt, chiles de árbol, and oregano. Spread 1 1/2 tablespoons of the topping across each enchilada. Top with the onion rings. If not serving right away, warm in a moderate oven for 15 to 20 minutes.

Creamy Green Enchiladas
Enchiladas Suizas

MAKES 12 ENCHILADAS

These enchiladas, called Swiss enchiladas because of their massive use of cheese and cream, were created at Sanborn's Café in Mexico City in the 1950s. It's an example of Mexican fusion cuisine at its best. Typically, these are chicken enchiladas, but my version uses artichoke hearts and zucchini, because they go insanely well with the creamy green sauce. For the best flavor, you'll want to make your own Salsa Verde (page 50), but if you're looking for ease, get a good-quality salsa verde, mix it with some cashew cream and vegan sour cream, and you've got an instant enchiladas suizas sauce.

Filling:
1 1/2 cups chopped jarred or fresh artichoke hearts (see note)

2 large zucchini, cut into 2 x 1/2-inch pieces

1 tablespoon Garlic-Citrus Olive Oil (page 43) or olive oil

1/2 teaspoon coarse sea salt

Sauce:
2 cups Salsa Verde (page 50) or store-bought salsa verde

1 cup vegan sour cream, whipped vigorously or 1/2 cup cashew cream
combined with 1/2 cup vegan sour cream

Tortillas and Toppings:
Corn oil, for frying

12 (6-inch) corn tortillas

2 cups shredded vegan white melting cheese

Garnishes:
1/4 cup chopped fresh cilantro

1/2 small white onion, sliced into 1/8-inch thick rings

Preheat the oven to 450°F. Toss the artichoke hearts, zucchini, Garlic-Citrus Olive Oil, and salt together in a 9 x 13-inch baking dish. Bake the artichoke mixture for 25 minutes, tossing again after 15 minutes, and transfer it to a medium mixing bowl. Lower the temperature of the oven to 350°F.

In a blender or food processor, purée the Salsa Verde and sour cream. Spread one-third of the sauce on the bottom of the 9 x 13-inch baking dish and set the remainder aside.

Add 1/4 inch of corn oil to a medium skillet and heat it to 350°F. Fry a tortilla in the oil for 3 seconds and transfer it to the baking dish. Fill it with about 3 tablespoons of the filling and roll it closed tightly. Repeat this process with the remaining tortillas and try to keep at least a 1/2-inch space between each enchilada. Smother the enchiladas in the remainder of the sauce. Top with the cheese. Bake the enchiladas for 20 minutes. Garnish each serving with the cilantro and onion rings.

Note: Replace any or all of the artichoke hearts and zucchini with up to 3 cups shredded vegan chicken strips.

Sweet Potato and Black Bean Mole Enchiladas
Enchiladas Mole de Frijoles Negro y Camotes Blancos

MAKES 12 ENCHILADAS

Moles are often considered the holy grail of Mexican sauces. Combine that with an enchilada and all I can say is that you chose wisely. These enchiladas balance the heat and deep resonant flavors of the mole Poblano with the umami qualities of black beans and the light sweetness of white sweet potatoes. If you want the best mole possible, use the recipe in this book to make your own (page 176), but if you're pressed for time, you can use the mole shortcut and still have enchiladas deliciosos.

Filling:
1 medium white sweet potato (see note)
3/4 cup Oaxacan-Style Black Beans (page 31) or cooked black beans

Sauce:
1 cup Mole Poblano (page 176)
3/4 cup water
1/4 teaspoon salt

Tortillas:
Corn oil, for frying
12 (6-inch) corn tortillas

Toppings:
3 tablespoons chopped fresh sage
1/4 cup chopped salted roasted peanuts

Preheat the oven to 450°F. Wrap the sweet potato in foil and bake it for 40 minutes. Once it is cool enough to handle, remove the foil and peel the sweet potato. Chop it into 1-inch chunks. Toss the sweet potato chunks with the Oaxacan-Style Black Beans and set aside.

In a medium skillet over medium-low heat, combine the Mole Poblano, water, and salt and warm the sauce.

Add 1/4 inch of oil to a deep skillet and heat it to just above medium heat. Place a plate near the sauce. Fry a tortilla in the oil for about 3 seconds, then submerge it in the sauce for about 10 seconds. Transfer the tortilla to the plate and add about 3 tablespoons of the filling. Roll the tortilla closed and transfer to a serving platter. Repeat this process with the remaining tortillas. Pour the remaining sauce over the enchiladas.

Drop the sage in the hot oil and fry it about 45 seconds, until it crisps. Remove it from the oil and sprinkle it on top of the enchiladas along with the peanuts.

Note: If you can't find a white sweet potato, you can substitute it with an orange sweet potato.

Miner's Enchiladas
Enchiladas Mineras

MAKES 12 ENCHILADAS

These cheese and onion enchiladas come from Guanajuato and are a regional riff on enchiladas rojas, utilizing a sauce made entirely of guajillo chiles and topped with lots of tasty veggies instead of being stuffed with them. If you're craving cheese enchiladas, these are absolutely the ones to make.

Toppings:
1 tablespoon corn or olive oil
3 medium Yukon gold potatoes, chopped into 1/2-inch pieces
2 medium carrots, cut into 1-inch long, 1/2-inch thick sticks
1/4 teaspoon coarse salt
1 cup shredded red leaf lettuce
Pickled jalapeños, to taste
1/2 cup Simple Queso Fresco (page 42) or 1/4 cup toasted pine nuts

Sauce:
6 guajillo chiles, stemmed, seeded, and rehydrated
2 cloves garlic
1/2 tablespoon dried Mexican oregano
1 teaspoon ground cumin
1 teaspoon salt
1 cup reserved chile water
2 to 3 chipotles in adobo, optional

Tortillas:
Corn oil, for frying
12 (6-inch) corn tortillas

Filling:
2 cups melting vegan white cheese
1 large white onion, minced and rinsed with cool water

Toppings: Heat the oil over medium-high heat in a medium skillet. Add the potatoes, carrots, and salt and sauté them until the potatoes are crisp and cooked through. Set aside.

Sauce: In a blender or food processor, purée the guajillos, garlic, Mexican oregano, cumin, salt, chile water, and chipotles in adobo (if using). Transfer the sauce to a large skillet and warm the sauce over low heat.

Tortillas: Add 1/4 inch of oil to an 8-inch (or larger) skillet and heat it to 375°F over medium heat. Place the warm sauce next to the skillet and place a dinner plate next to the sauce. Fry a tortilla in the oil for 3 seconds and immediately dip it into the sauce for about 5 seconds. Transfer the tortilla to the plate. Fill the tortilla with about 1/4 cup of the filling and roll it or fold it closed. Transfer it to a serving platter. Repeat this process with the remaining tortillas.

Pour any remaining sauce over the top of the enchiladas and top with the potato mixture, lettuce, pickled jalapeños, and Simple Queso Fresco or toasted pine nuts.

TAMALES

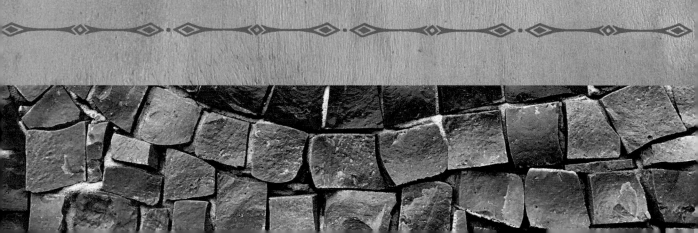

Tamales are one of those foods that make most people say, "Yes, please!" I will stop what I'm doing if someone puts a well-done tamale in front of me—a fluffy light morsel filled with a spicy and succulent filling that slowly releases its corn-scented steam as I carefully unwrap it.

There's a reason tamales have been around since at least 5,000 BCE—they're delicious!—though they didn't take their more modern form until Mesoamerican people learned how to nixtamalize corn. In fact, ancient tamales were, in all likelihood, pit-roasted and not steamed, and they weren't necessarily made with any dough at all.

The word "tamale" is the Spanish spelling of the Nahuatl word "tamalli," which simply means "wrapped." You can still see the descendants of these primal tamales in modern Mexico, where grilled and roasted tamales can still be found (a few made without masa can be found, as well). Even in tamales that use masa, which is nearly all of them now, the types of tamales available are so numerous, several large books could be dedicated to them. There are the standard green chile tamales, tamales filled with chilorio, tamales folded in banana leaves and roasted pibil-style (i.e., cooked in the ground), tiny tamales that are one-bite affairs, and even a giant tamale made for festivals that comes in at over six feet long! For those who want tamale flavors, but don't want to go through the effort of making them, there is even a tamale casserole: cazuela de tamales.

Tamales have a reputation for being labor-intensive and time-consuming. A good tamale does take time, but nearly all of that is letting the masa rest and steaming the tamales. I find tamales only become labor-intensive if I am making big batches of fifty or more. They're very easy if you choose a simple filling and put your tamales together in assembly-line fashion. When I make batches, I line up my corn husks or banana leaves, spread the masa on all of them, and only then fill them. Once they're filled, I roll them. When you get going like this, it's amazing how quickly they go. That being said, I highly suggest inviting friends and family over to help make them. That's how it's traditionally done, and it's a lot of fun to throw a tamale party.

Masa for Tamales

Just like there are a variety of tamales, they can be made with different doughs. Some are denser than others, and some are even made out of rice and other starchy ingredients like fresh corn. However, the most common masa for tamales is the one presented here. If prepared properly, it's light and airy, and your tamales will turn out fluffy. That's what most of us crave when we think tamales. You'll want to pay attention to each of the techniques and the way the ingredients are prepped. It's easy to make decent masa for tamales, but it takes practice, precision, and patience to make it outstanding.

Masa is best after it rests one hour, which gives the dry particles plenty of time to absorb the liquid. Make sure your shortening is chilled. The shortening combines better with the masa if it gets whipped in cold, because it creates tiny pockets in the dough, similar to a puff pastry but on a tinier scale. These mini-pockets of fat melt when the tamale cooks, leaving the pockets in place and creating a fluffy texture. Finally, you can do this by hand if you prefer, but it's best to use a stand mixer to do the heavy mixing. It will spare your arm and make a lighter tamale.

> **1 3/4 cups masa harina**
> **1 1/2 teaspoons salt**
> **1 teaspoon baking powder**
> **1 1/2 cups hot water**
> **3/4 cup chilled vegan shortening**

In a stand mixer, evenly combine the masa harina, salt, and baking powder. Turn the machine on to low speed and slowly pour in the hot water. Once all the water is added, increase the speed to medium and let it whip the masa for 10 minutes. Cover with plastic wrap and refrigerate for 1 hour.

Return the masa to the stand mixer and mix the masa at high speed for 5 minutes. Add the shortening 2 to 3 tablespoons at a time. Once all the shortening has been added, continue beating the masa for 20 minutes.

If you want to add some extra flavor to the masa, it's easy to create a flavored broth that replaces the water. Here are a few different broths you can use. Each broth uses 1 1/2 cups of water to keep the amount of liquid the same:

- **Sweet Broth:** Melt 1 ounce of piloncillo or brown sugar into the water.
- **Chile-Flavored Broth:** Add 2 tablespoons guajillo or ancho chile powder and 1 1/2 teaspoons Mexican oregano to the water and make sure they dissolve.
- **Achiote-Flavored Broth:** Dissolve 1 tablespoon achiote paste into the hot water.
- **Roasted Garlic–Flavored Broth:** Purée 10 cloves roasted garlic with the water, then heat.

Filling Tamales

I like my tamales well-filled, so I use about 1 1/2 tablespoons filling per tamale. Place the filling in a line down the center of the tamale, but leave some space at the top and bottom so the filling doesn't spill out those ends when you fold the tamale closed. You can increase or decrease the filling amount and you'll want to conversely decrease or increase the amount of masa you use.

Wrapping Tamales

Corn husks are the most common wrapper used, but you can also make a great (and very large) tamale by wrapping it in a banana leaf. The banana leaf will alter the shape of the tamale and impart a slight herbal note to the masa. I get inexpensive banana leaves at both my local Mexican and Asian markets and dried corn husks are available just about everywhere. There are also specialty tamales wrapped in other leaves, like the hoja santa leaf. These leaves are about as large as a corn husk and a tamale steamed in an hoja santa leaf will have a unique, fragrant, light quality to it.

Corn Husk: To wrap a tamale in a corn husk, soak the husks in hot water for about 30 minutes to soften them. Spread the masa across the husk, leaving 3/4 inch of the husk clear on both sides, 1 1/2 inches clear on the top, and 2 1/2 inches clear at the bottom. I prefer thick tamales, so I usually spread the masa about 1/3-inch thick. If you prefer more filling than masa, you can spread the masa 1/4-inch thick. I know some people who spread their masa 1/2-inch thick, but that's a little too much masa for my tastes. Experiment and find what you like.

Add the filling in the middle of the tamale and fold up the sides, placing one side above the other to enclose the filling. Gently roll the tamale closed by tucking one end of the husk under the other, pressing the masa back a bit. Avoid rolling the tamales like a jelly roll, so the husk doesn't get stuck in the masa. Tuck the bottom pointy side of the husk under the tamale. Twist the end of the husk closed and tie the ends with strips of corn husk, or simply leave them as is.

Banana Leaf: The proportions for using banana leaves, which are more commonly used in the tropical regions of Mexico, are similar, but you want a large banana leaf so you can leave about 3 inches clear on all sides. To prepare the banana leaves, cut them so they are relatively square. Steam or boil them for about 5 minutes so that they are pliable. Add the masa in the same proportions as detailed earlier, fold two opposite sides together, then the other opposite sides, making a rectangular packet. Gently tie the packet closed with banana leaf strips or twine.

Filling a husk tamale

Filling a banana leaf tamale

Cooking Tamales

Steaming is the most popular way to cook tamales, but you can also boil and even grill them. For something a little off-beat, try grilling them. You'll be pleasantly surprised.

Steaming is by far the most common method of cooking tamales. (Steamed tamales are also known as vaporcitos.) There are steamers made specifically for tamales, and if you plan on making tamales often, it's worth purchasing one. However, you can also use a simple bamboo steamer. By standing your tamales vertically, you'll be able to fit more in the steamer. Stand them with the folded bottom down. If you can't stand them, layer them in one layer in your steaming basket. To make a lot of tamales, use a steaming basket with multiple layers. I rotate the layers every 10 minutes to ensure that all the tamales cook evenly. Be careful when you do this, so you don't end up with steamed hands.

Ideally, the tamales should be gently steamed for 45 minutes. Once your pan or steamer begins to steam, reduce the heat to medium-low. If you leave the heat very high, the bottoms of your tamales will overcook. Make sure the steamer is covered so the heat and moisture can fully permeate the masa. Once the tamales have steamed, you can store them for later use or serve them immediately. Let them sit for about 5 minutes after steaming to rest the masa and so that they cool enough to handle.

Tamales aren't normally grilled, but grilling was the original way to make them. I like certain tamales grilled, most notably those from Yucatán. If you grill your tamales, you'll want to add an extra corn husk or banana leaf to protect the tamale. Let your coals die down to a medium-low heat or light a gas grill to the same temperature. If using coals, nestle the tamales directly in the coals. Alternatively, you can place them on the grill rack. Just make sure the rack is close to the heat. Cook the tamales for 1 hour, flipping them halfway through.

Boiling tamales will make the masa dense and wet, but it's an opportunity to infuse it with a sauce. You can flavor the boiling water with salt, dried chiles, oregano, cumin, pepper, cinnamon, achiote, garlic, on-

ion, or anything else that you want to infuse in your tamales. Just make sure the boiling liquid is strongly flavored. Gently boil the tamales for about 3 hours, replenishing the liquid as necessary.

Basic Recipes

Following are several recipes for tamales, most of which are fillings that you can use with the basic masa recipe on page 120. You can use any of the cooking techniques with these recipes, though most people prefer them steamed. In addition, I've included a few specific tamale recipes that defy the guidelines I've already presented, like the tamale casserole. You can make your tamales as thick or as thin as you like. Keep in mind that the more masa you use, the fewer tamales you'll have, and if you like extra-thin masa, you'll want to increase the amount of filling you make. The amount of filling for these recipes assumes you are using a 1/3-inch thick masa spread on a standard-size corn husk. If you end up with extra filling, that's not a bad thing, as these fillings make great taco fillings, too. Now you know what to do with the leftovers. Expect these recipes to make 12 to 18 tamales, depending on how much masa you use per tamale.

Classic Red Tamales
Tamales de Chilorio

1 batch Masa for Tamales (page 120)
1 1/2 cups Mushroom Chilorio using mushrooms or shredded seitan (page 169)

Veracruz-Inspired Tamales
Tamales Estilo Veracruz

1 batch Masa for Tamales (page 120)
2 ancho chiles, fried or toasted and rehydrated
8 pitted brine-cured green olives stuffed with garlic, finely chopped
1/4 cup raisins
1/4 cup roasted salted pepitas
1/3 cup cooked black beans or shredded seitan

Cut the chiles into 1/4-inch dice. Toss the chiles, green olives, raisins, pepitas, and beans or seitan together in a medium bowl.

Green Chile and Corn Tamales
Tamales de Chiles Verdes y Elotes

1 batch Masa for Tamales (page 120)
3/4 cup fresh corn kernels
1 cup coarsely chopped roasted green chiles, like poblanos or Hatch chiles
1/2 cup Simple Queso Fresco (page 42) or your favorite vegan cheese

Once the masa is ready, mix the corn kernels into the masa. Combine the chiles and cheese for the filling.

Pit-Roasted Mushroom Tamales
Tamales Pibil de Hongos

2 teaspoons achiote paste

1 batch Masa for Tamales (page 120)

1 cup diced cremini mushrooms or oyster mushrooms

1/2 teaspoon salt

1/2 teaspoon freshly ground black pepper

2 tablespoons chopped fresh epazote

Mix the achiote paste with the masa as you are whipping it. Combine the mushrooms, salt, pepper, and epazote for the filling. Wrap the assembled tamales in banana leaves (preferably) or corn husks and cook using the grilling method.

Sweet Tamales
Tamales de Dulce

6 tablespoons sugar
1 1/2 cups hot water
6 drops red food coloring
1 3/4 cups masa harina
1 1/2 teaspoons salt
1 teaspoon baking powder
3/4 cup chilled vegan shortening
1/2 cup raisins

Melt the sugar in the hot water and add the food coloring.

In a stand mixer, evenly combine the masa harina, salt, and baking powder. Turn the machine on to low speed and slowly pour in the hot water mixture. Once all the water is added, increase the speed to medium and let it whip the masa for 10 minutes. Cover with plastic wrap and refrigerate for 1 hour.

Return the masa to the stand mixer and mix the masa at high speed for 5 minutes. Add the shortening 2 to 3 tablespoons at a time. Once all the shortening has been added, continue beating the masa for 20 minutes.

Once the masa is ready, mix the raisins into it. These tamales are all masa, with no filling, so spread the masa at least 1-inch thick.

Apple Tamales
Tamales de Manzanas

3 medium green apples, cored and cut into 1/4-inch pieces
1/4 teaspoon salt
1 batch Masa for Tamales (page 120)

In a medium bowl, combine the apples, and salt. Prepare the tamales using the masa for tamales and fill each tamale with apple filling.

Potato-Chorizo Tamales
Tamales de Papas y Chorizo

1 batch Masa for Tamales (page 120)
2 medium russet potatoes, peeled and cut into 1/4-inch dice
1/3 teaspoon salt
1/2 cup Red Chorizo (page 40)

Toss the potatoes with the salt, then combine them with the Red Chorizo for the filling. If you grill these tamales, you will need to steam the diced potatoes for 7 to 8 minutes first.

Large Tamales
with Black-Eyed Peas
Pimes

MAKES 2 TAMALES

These tamales are a specialty of Yucatán that I first learned about from author David Sterling. They're fairly large tamales and require banana leaves to make. They are filled with a mix of ground pepitas and, traditionally, hard-boiled eggs. I replace the eggs with sliced avocado. What makes these tamales extra special is that the masa is flavored with achiote paste and black-eyed peas are mixed into it. Each tamale serves 4 to 5 people. Note: This recipe uses banana leaves instead of corn husks.

    1 tablespoon achiote paste
    1 batch Masa for Tamales (page 120), modified (see below)
    1 cup cooked black-eyed peas, rinsed
    2 roasted Roma tomatoes
    1/2 cup salted roasted pepitas
    1 ripe Hass avocado, pitted, peeled, and sliced
    Crushed Red Salsa (page 48), for serving
    Shredded green cabbage, for serving

Mix the achiote paste into the masa as you are whipping it. Once you are done whipping it, mix the black eyed peas into the masa by hand. Lay out banana leaves to make 2 tamales. Make sure you have enough banana leaves that you can close them around a 7- to 8-inch disc. Form two (7- to 8-inch diameter) discs of masa on the banana leaves, using half the batch of masa. In a blender or food processor, purée the tomatoes and pepitas. Spread the tomato mixture on the discs, then layer on the sliced avocado.

Form 2 more discs from the remaining masa and lay these on top of the tamales. Gently use your palm to close the sides of the tamales and enclose them in the banana leaves. Tie the tamales closed with twine or strips of banana leaf.

Cook these using the grill method or bake them at 350°F for 45 minutes. Slice them into 4 or 5 pieces per tamale and serve with the Crushed Red Salsa and cabbage on the side.

Tamales de Costeños and No-Fat Tamales

Tamales de Costeños, or tamales made on the coast, are often wrapped in banana leaves, and the masa tends to be denser than the more common tamale. You only whip the masa for 10 minutes, and you can add half as much shortening or even omit it entirely. These tamales are meant to be substantial meals, so a dense masa is desirable. However, you want to spread the masa a bit thin so the tamales don't feel too dense.

Fresh Corn Tamales
Tamales de Elotes Frescas

These tamales are fascinating to me, because they're not made with masa, they're made with puréed fresh corn. This corn purée is mixed with a little masa harina to help bind the tamales, but the majority of tamale is made from sweet, fresh corn. Make sure the corn is in season when you make these; otherwise, they will turn out lackluster. You can top them with whatever you like, but this version is my favorite.

6 cups fresh corn kernels, husks reserved
1/4 cup vegan butter
1 teaspoon salt
1/2 cup masa harina
Salsa Verde (page 50), for serving
Roasted Chile Strips (page 39), for serving
Simple Queso Fresco (page 42), for serving

In a blender or food processor, purée the corn kernels, butter, and salt. Transfer the corn mixture to a medium bowl and combine it with the masa harina. Use fresh corn husks as your wrappers and fill them with approximately 1/2 cup of the masa filling. Fold each tamale closed and steam or grill them.

Tamale Casserole
Cazuela de Tamal

MAKES 4 TO 6 SERVINGS

This is an easy way to the flavors of a tamale with little effort. It uses a cazuela, but you can use any sort of wide, deep pan if you don't have a cazuela available. This makes a great family dinner, and you can make it a day ahead of time if you like.

Corn or olive oil
1 batch Masa for Tamales (page 120, see note)
2 medium Yukon gold potatoes, cut into 1-inch dice
1 1/2 cups cooked white beans (any kind), rinsed
1 1/2 cups Salsa Verde (page 50)

Preheat the oven to 375°F. Lightly oil a 12-inch cazuela, iron skillet, or oven-proof pan. Take half the masa and spread it around the bottom and up the sides of the cooking vessel. Fill it with the potatoes, beans, and Salsa Verde. Take the remaining half of the masa and cover the filling, pinching it closed at the rim. Bake for 45 minutes. Serve with extra Salsa Verde if you like.

Note: You don't need to whip this masa if you don't mind a thick dough, which seems to work better with this dish than with a traditional tamale.

Tamales in Peanut-Tequila Mole
Tamales en Encacahuatado

MAKES 4 TO 6 SERVINGS

This is the fancy tamale you serve to impress your guests. Plus, the mole is amazing and can be used in other recipes. It takes a little time and a lot of ingredients to make the mole, so I suggest making a double or triple batch so you have leftovers. It's a beautiful, if complicated, tamale.

Tamales:
1 batch Masa for Tamales (page 120)
1 small russet potato, cut into 1/4-inch pieces
1/2 cup shredded canned, water-packed jackfruit or seitan
Juice of 2 limes
1 tablespoon guajillo chile powder
1/4 cup raisins
3/4 teaspoon salt

Peanut-Tequila Mole:
1 tablespoon plus 1/4 cup olive oil, divided
1/2 medium white onion, cut into 1/4-inch dice
3 cloves garlic, minced
3 ancho chiles, toasted or fried, rehydrated, and stemmed
4 roasted Roma tomatoes
2 chipotles in adobo
1 cup roasted salted peanuts
1/8 teaspoon ground allspice
1/2 teaspoon ground cinnamon
1/2 teaspoon freshly ground black pepper
1 teaspoon salt
1 tablespoon sugar
1 dried bay leaf
Juice of 2 limes
1/4 cup tequila blanco
3 cups vegetable broth

Tamales: Prepare the masa and set aside. In a bowl, combine the potato, jackfruit, lime juice, chile powder, raisins, and salt for the filling. Assemble the tamales and steam them. While they are steaming, make the mole.

Peanut-Tequila Mole: Heat 1 tablespoon of the oil in a medium skillet over medium heat. Add the onion and cook until it just starts to brown, about 5 minutes. Add the garlic and cook 2 more minutes. Transfer the onion mixture to a blender, along with the anchos, tomatoes, chipotles, peanuts, allspice, cinnamon, pepper, salt, sugar, bay leaf, lime juice, tequila blanco, and broth. Purée the onion mixture until it is smooth.

Add the remaining 1/4 cup oil to the skillet. Once the oil is hot, add the mole and cook for 30 minutes, stirring occasionally, until it is thick. Serve the tamales unwrapped and spoon 2 tablespoons of mole over each tamale.

Chilled Chayote Salad (page 142)

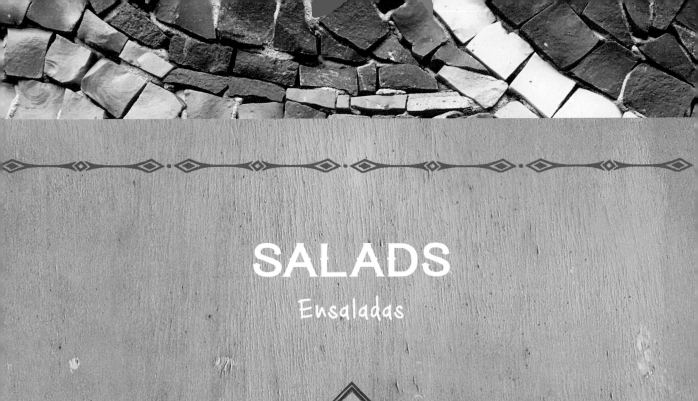

SALADS

Ensaladas

The abundance of fresh fruits and vegetables has gone a long way toward making the salad an all-star course. Once you start delving into Mexican cuisine, you'll discover just how loco para ensaladas *we are!*

We don't often see the fresh side of Mexican cuisine, and that's a shame. One of the biggest misconceptions about Mexican food is that it's a grease-laden morass of cheese smothered in super-spicy salsa. While those recipes certainly exist, the misconception is exacerbated by restaurants outside of Mexico. In truth, it's hard to find a Mexican cocina without fresh greens and vegetables. Salads like to make an appearance either before or alongside a main dish. And they're not just leafy greens. There are salads made from avocados, mangos, cactus, and squash.

If you have some fresh fruits or vegetables sitting around, chop them up and think of ways you can add flavor components to them. For hard vegetables, simmer them for a few minutes to make them al dente (never mushy). Find ways to enhance flavors by adding fresh radishes or chiles and herbs like epazote, cilantro, parsley, and sage. Using citrus will add pop and zest to your salad. For crunch, add items like pepitas, peanuts, or walnuts. For sweetness, add grapes. For creaminess, avocado is the go-to ingredient. Once you start playing around with those ingredients and thinking about ways you can add layers of texture and flavor, you'll be on your way to crafting your own Mexican salads.

"Ensalada" usually refers to a salad made with leafy greens, but there are plenty of other salads named simply for their main ingredients. In order to show the versatility and veggie-richness of many Mexican dishes, I use the word "ensalada" to encompass all those dishes.

Watermelon Jicama Salad

Ensalada de Sandia y Jicama

MAKES 4 SERVINGS

Fruit and chiles go hand-in-hand in Mexico, from the spicy tequila chaser sangrita to sticks of fresh fruit dressed with chiles and lime sold from the ubiquitous food carts. Fresh sweet fruits and melons make for a refreshing afternoon respite, and spicy chiles add a little perk to your step. When watermelon season comes around, this salad becomes a weekly tradition at my house. It only takes minutes to put together and explodes with a wide variety of flavors and textures, all from just a few ingredients. Fresh, sweet, hot, crunchy, salty, lively, this salad has everything I crave.

2 cups 1/2-inch diced watermelon
2 cups 1/2-inch diced peeled jicama
Juice of 2 limes
3 tablespoons salted roasted pepitas
1 tablespoon minced fresh mint
1 tablespoon guajillo chile powder
1/2 teaspoon pequín chile powder, optional
1/3 teaspoon coarse sea salt

Combine the watermelon, jicama, lime juice, pepitas, mint, guajillo chile powder, pequín chile powder (if using), and salt in a medium bowl, let the salad sit for 5 minutes, and serve.

Mango Avocado Salad

Ensalada de Mango y Aguacate

MAKES 4 SERVINGS

Fruit and avocados are combined in so many different salads in Mexico, but this combination is one of my favorites. It's a simple mix of sweet mango, lush avocado, tangy lime juice, and pepita crunch. Add serrano chiles to your tongue's delight!

3 cups coarsely chopped mango

2 ripe Hass avocados, pitted, peeled, and chopped

Juice of 2 limes

1/4 teaspoon salt

1/4 cup salted roasted pepitas

Minced seeded serrano chiles, to taste

Combine the mango, avocados, lime juice, salt, pepitas, and serranos (if using) in a medium bowl. Let the salad rest for about 5 minutes and serve.

Morelos-Style Fruit Salad

Gazpacho Moreliano

MAKES 4 SERVINGS

This fruit salad is usually served in a glass, and while it may be called gazpacho, it's not like the puréed Spanish gazpacho you may be familiar with. Instead, this salad layers fruit, cheese, and onion and swims in a simple citrus-chile dressing. You can use your favorite crumbly vegan cheese, make it with pine nuts, or use fruit only. The options are many for this street salad. You can even be a little naughty and add a shot of tequila to the dressing. Make it your own!

1 cup peeled and diced jicama

1 cup diced mango

1 cup diced pineapple

1 cup peeled and diced cucumber

1/2 small white onion, minced and rinsed with cool water

1/4 cup Simple Queso Fresco (page 42) or pine nuts

1 cup fresh orange juice

1/4 cup fresh lime juice

1/8 teaspoon salt

Chile pequín powder or chile powder of your choice, to taste

2 tablespoons tequila, optional

Combine the jicama, mango, and pineapple in a medium bowl. In a separate bowl, combine the cucumber and onion. In two small glasses, add one quarter of the jicama mixture to each glass. Next, add one quarter of the cucumber mixture, then add one quarter of the cheese or nuts. Repeat the layering process.

Combine the orange juice, lime juice, salt, chile powder, and tequila (if using) in a small bowl. Pour the dressing into the glasses, dividing it equally. Serve the salad immediately, or cover and refrigerate for up to 4 hours.

Cactus Salad

Ensalada de Nopalitos Mexicana

MAKES 3 TO 4 SERVINGS

This salad is quintessentially Mexican not only because it uses cactus, tomatoes, and cheese but also because those three ingredients represent the three colors of the Mexican flag. It's one of the most popular salads found in Mexico, and it's often served as a starter to a meal. I frequently substitute avocado for the vegan cheese. It's quicker, healthier, and simple. You'll want to make sure to use fresh cactus, not the jarred kind, which many Mexican markets carry. If you can't find that, try making the salad with sautéed strips of zucchini or simply make the Spanish Salad on page 139.

- 3 cactus paddles, trimmed and cut into 1-inch pieces (about 2 cups)
- Water, as needed
- 1 1/4 teaspoons salt, divided
- 1 tablespoon red wine vinegar
- 3 Roma tomatoes, seeded and chopped into 1-inch pieces
- 3 cebollitas (also known as knob onions), sliced paper thin, or 1 small white onion, sliced paper thin
- 1 cup cubed Simple Queso Fresco (page 42) or 2 ripe Hass avocados, pitted, peeled, and chopped
- 1/4 cup chopped fresh cilantro
- 1 teaspoon dried oregano

Submerge the cactus in a bowl with enough water to cover. Add 1 teaspoon of the salt, stir, and let the cactus sit for 30 minutes.

Drain the cactus. In a small pot, add the cactus and cover it with fresh water. Add the vinegar. Bring the cactus to a simmer and cook 5 minutes, then drain. Toss the cactus with the tomatoes, cebollitas or onion, Simple Queso Fresco or avocados, cilantro, the remaining 1/4 teaspoon salt, and oregano and serve immediately.

Spanish Salad

Ensalada de Española

MAKES 3 TO 4 SERVINGS

The olive oil and lemon dressing really showcases the Spanish influence in this salad, and it's a fantastic alternative to its cousin, the Cactus Salad (page 138). I make this version when I don't feel like searching for fresh cactus. The key to this salad is using in-season tomatoes and avocados that aren't too ripe. They should have just a tiny amount of give when you squeeze them.

> **3 Roma tomatoes, seeded and cut into 1-inch pieces**
> **1/2 small white onion, minced and rinsed with cool water**
> **2 barely ripe large Hass avocados, pitted, peeled, and chopped**
> **2 tablespoons olive oil**
> **Juice of 1 large lemon or 2 small lemons**
> **1/2 teaspoon freshly cracked black pepper**
> **1 teaspoon minced fresh oregano**

Combine the tomatoes, onion, avocados, oil, lemon juice, pepper, and oregano in a bowl and serve immediately.

Christmas Eve Salad

Ensalada de Noche Buena

MAKES 5 TO 6 SERVINGS

My mom used to make this salad, but I had no idea it was a traditional Mexican Christmas Eve salad. I'm not even sure my mom knew. It was just something the family did. There are so many variations on it that I could recite a hundred different versions, but at its heart, it's a colorful fruit salad using in-season ingredients and almost always features citrus. I love it, and I'll eat it any time of year.

Salad:
1 small beet, sliced into 1/4-inch thick discs
Water, as needed
2 cups baby arugula
1 orange, peeled and sliced into 1/4-inch thick discs
1 medium green apple, diced into 1/2-inch pieces
1 very small jicama, peeled and diced into 1/2-inch pieces
1 ripe plantain, peeled and chopped into 3/4-inch pieces
1/3 cup salted roasted peanuts or pepitas

Dressing:
Juice of 1 orange
Juice of 1 lime
3 to 4 tablespoons beet water
1 (2-inch) piece piloncillo or 2 tablespoons brown sugar melted into simmering liquid, optional
Crushed chiles de árbol, to taste, optional

Simmer the beet slices in a small saucepan with enough water to cover over medium heat until just soft, about 4 minutes, then remove from the heat. Remove the beets, set aside, and reserve the simmering liquid for use in the dressing. Combine the beets, arugula, orange, apple, jicama, plantain, and peanuts or pepitas in a salad bowl or nicely arrange them on a platter. In a small bowl, combine the orange juice, lime juice, beet water, piloncillo or brown sugar (if using), and crushed chiles de árbol (is using). Let the dressing come to room temperature and pour it over the salad. Serve immediately.

To make this ahead of time, leave out the arugula until you are ready to serve, then combine it with the other salad ingredients.

Chilled Chayote Salad
Ensalada de Chayote

MAKES 3 TO 4 SERVINGS

This simple salad can serve as an entire lunch on its own or as a side dish for a larger meal. The chayotes are hearty and this normally bland squash takes on a delectable flavor once it simmers in salted water. It's best if the salad can rest for at least an hour before serving, assuming you have the patience to let it sit that long. I usually don't.

- 3 medium chayotes, chopped into 1-inch pieces
- Water, as needed
- 1 teaspoon salt
- 1 teaspoon minced fresh oregano or 3/4 teaspoon dried oregano
- 1 to 2 serrano chiles, seeded and minced
- 1/4 small red onion, minced
- 2 tablespoons Garlic-Citrus Olive Oil (page 43), garlic olive oil, or plain olive oil
- 2 tablespoons red wine vinegar

In a medium saucepan, cover the chayotes with water, add the salt, and bring the water to a simmer. Simmer the chayotes until they are just soft, about 8 to 10 minutes. Drain and quickly transfer to a salad bowl, then immediately toss the chayotes with the oregano, serranos, and red onion. Whisk the Garlic-Citrus Olive Oil and vinegar together and dress the salad. Let the salad sit for 1 hour and serve either at room temperature or slightly chilled.

Variation: Swap zucchinis for chayotes. Instead of chayotes, you can make this salad with zucchinis, Mexican gray squash, or even green apples. If you use the alternative squash, simmer until it is just soft. If you use the apples, toss them with a sprinkle of salt and leave them fresh instead of cooking them.

Spinach-Potato Salad
with Lime-Agave Dressing

Ensalada de Espinacas y Papas en Salsa de Agave y Lima

MAKES 3 SERVINGS

Mexico is replete with potato salads and spinach salads, so why not combine the two? This salad features the best of both worlds, with al dente potatoes, fresh spinach, and sautéed poblanos and onions in a sweet and sour dressing, with an optional chorizo addition for good measure. Add some beans and make it a meal on its own. This salad is also great the next day.

2 teaspoons olive oil

2 poblano chiles, seeded and cut into 3/4-inch pieces

1 small red onion, sliced into 1/8-inch thick strips

4 small Yukon gold potatoes, cut into 1/2-inch dice

Water, as needed

1 teaspoon salt

4 cups baby spinach leaves

Zest of 2 limes

Juice of 2 limes

1 tablespoon agave syrup

1/2 teaspoon coarsely ground black pepper

1/2 cup Red Chorizo (page 40), optional

Heat the oil in a medium skillet over medium heat. Add the poblanos and onion and sauté until the onion has just started to brown, 6 to 8 minutes.

Put the potatoes in a small pot and cover with the water, then add the salt. Bring the potatoes to a simmer and cook until the potatoes are al dente, 5 to 6 minutes. Drain and immediately toss with the spinach.

Combine the lime zest, lime juice, and agave. Combine the poblano mixture, potato mixture, and chorizo (if using) and toss with the Lime-Agave Dressing.

Time-Saving Tip: Simmer the potatoes while you sauté the poblanos and onion and mix the dressing while the poblanos and onion are cooking.

Green Pozole (page 150)

SOUPS

Sopas y Caldos

Who doesn't love a good soup? A pot of simmering beans or chiles, redolent with cinnamon and cloves and garlic and onions, or the simple scent of cooking greens and corn makes me want to find an excuse to hang out in the kitchen with those wonderful aromas.

A good Mexican soup finds a balance between flavors that dance around the tongue and a feeling of hominess. It's comfort food for the soul and an adventure for the palate. The Oaxacan Chile Masa Soup (page 147) captures all those elements.

I'm assuming that you have figured out that "sopa" simply means "soup," but you may be wondering what a caldo is. A caldo is really just a hot, brothy soup or stew. Caldos are sopas, but not all sopas are caldos. Caldos are the types of soups I eat when I want to feel satisfied, but not heavy. They're great to serve alongside a main dish or as a hold-me-over between meals.

Fava Bean Soup
Sopa de Habas

MAKES 5 SERVINGS

This easy soup, traditionally served during Lent, is full of rich, deep caramelized flavors from sautéed onions, garlic, and tomatoes. The key is cooking everything down to make sure all the flavors are intensified. You can also make this with pinto beans instead of fava beans. Nopales make a frequent appearance in this soup, but if you don't have fresh nopales, simply omit them.

- 1 tablespoon olive oil
- 1 medium yellow onion, coarsely chopped
- 5 cloves garlic, coarsely chopped
- 4 Roma tomatoes
- 3 1/2 cups cooked fava beans, divided
- 2 cups water
- 1/2 teaspoon ground cumin
- 3/4 teaspoon salt
- 1 to 2 chipotles in adobo, minced
- 1 cup sliced nopales, optional

Heat the oil in a medium pot over medium heat. Add the onion and sauté until it is well caramelized, about 15 minutes. Add the garlic and sauté 2 more minutes. Add the tomatoes and cook until they are reduced, 7 to 8 minutes. Transfer the onion mixture to a blender, along with 1 cup of the fava beans, water, cumin, salt, and chipotles and purée. Transfer the purée back to the pot and add the remaining 2 1/2 cups fava beans and nopales (if using). Simmer the soup for 8 to 10 minutes and serve.

Oaxacan Chile Masa Soup
Chileatole Oaxaqueño

MAKES 6 TO 8 SERVINGS

Chileatole is the simple purée of chiles thickened with masa that's eaten all over central Mexico, especially during the winter. This particular version comes from Oaxaca, but most other versions of chileatole are fairly similar, perhaps adding something other than corn or substituting a different type of dried red chile. It's easy to put together and gently warming—Mexican comfort food at its best.

1 tablespoon oil

1 medium white or yellow onion, cut into 1/4-inch dice

3 cups fresh corn kernels

3 cloves garlic, minced

3 ancho or guajillo chiles (or a mix of both), stemmed, seeded, and rehydrated

6 cups water (use as much of the chile water as possible and add fresh water to make 6 cups)

1 cup masa harina

1 1/2 teaspoons salt

2 tablespoons minced fresh epazote, optional

2 cups chopped oyster mushrooms or 6 squash blossoms, optional

Heat the oil in a 3-quart pot over medium heat. Add the onion and corn and sauté until the onion lightly browns, 8 to 10 minutes. Add the garlic and cook 2 minutes. In a blender or food processor, purée the chiles with the water, masa harina, and salt. Add the purée to the pot with the epazote (if using), bring to a simmer, and cook for 4 to 5 minutes. Add the oyster mushrooms (if using). If using the squash blossoms, ladel the soup into serving bowls and then immediately add a squash blossom to each bowl.

Red Pozole
Pozole Rojo

MAKES 8 SERVINGS

When I think of Mexican soups, pozole always comes to mind. Plumped corn in an onion-chile broth is hard to beat. Add to that tostadas, limes, fresh radish, and cabbage, and it is over-the-top good. It's a celebration food popular all over Mexico and the American Southwest, but pozole has a sordid history. According to the Universidad Nacional Autónoma de México, the meat in the original pozole came from ritually sacrificed humans. Once the Spanish arrived, cannibalism wouldn't do, and pork became the meat of choice. My "meat" of choice is jackfruit and pinto beans, no sacrifices needed. Whenever anyone questions the authenticity of my vegan versions of classic dishes, I put on a wry grin and tell them the story of pozole. **Note:** Pozole is also called hominy and partially cooked pozole is called nixtamal para pozole.

Pozole Soup:
4 cups water, plus more as needed
6 cloves garlic, cut in half lengthwise
1 medium white onion, diced into 1/4-inch pieces
1 1/4 teaspoons salt
1 cup dried pozole or 1 (15-ounce) can hominy (pozole), rinsed (for Quick Version)
3/4 cup dried pinto beans or 1 (15-ounce) can pinto beans, rinsed (for Quick Version)
1 cup shredded water-packed canned jackfruit
3 ancho chiles, stemmed and seeded, or 1/4 cup ancho chile powder (for Quick Version)

Condiments (arranged in bowls around the Pozole):
2 tablespoons dried Mexican oregano
8 lime wedges
3 radishes, sliced paper thin
1 1/2 cups shredded cabbage
Tostadas or corn chips
Coarsely ground chiles de árbol

Bring the water to a simmer over medium heat in a 3-quart pot. Add the garlic, onion, salt, and dried pozole. Slowly simmer for 4 to 5 hours, replenishing the water as needed to keep it at about 6 cups. An hour before the soup is done simmering, add the dried beans and jackfruit, again replenishing the water as needed to keep it at 6 cups. While the soup is simmering, rehydrate the anchos. In a blender or food processor, purée the rehydrated anchos with 1 cup of the soup broth. Press this mixture through a fine-meshed sieve for the best texture. Add to the soup and simmer 10 minutes, then serve with the oregano, lime wedges, radishes, cabbage, tostadas or corn chips, and ground chiles de árbol. (The Mexican oregano should be crushed by rubbing it between your hands above the soup bowls.)

Quick Version: Simmer the water, garlic, onion, salt, and jackfruit for 10 minutes, add the canned pozole, canned beans, and ancho chile powder. Simmer for 5 more minutes and serve.

Green Pozole
Pozole Verde

MAKES 8 SERVINGS

This is a lighter, spicier version of the classic pozole rojo, and it's a favorite in Geurrero. It's made from pepitas, tomatillos, and lots of fresh green herbs (hence the name.) Its flavor is refreshing, bright, and highly addictive. What takes it over the edge for me is the simple addition of chopped avocado as a garnish. This recipe uses herbs most commonly found at a Mexican market, such as hoja santa and epazote, and I have included instructions for what to do if you can't find those.

Soup:
8 to 10 tomatillos, husked
4 cups water, plus more as needed for simmering
1/2 cup toasted salted pepitas
1 serrano chile, seeded and roughly chopped
1 hoja santa leaf (preferable) or 10 sorrel leaves, optional
2 to 3 tablespoons corn or olive oil
1 tablespoon chopped fresh epazote (preferable) or cilantro
1 teaspoon salt
1 large chayote or Mexican gray squash, coarsely chopped
2 cups cooked hominy (pozole)
1 1/2 cups cooked white beans (any kind)

Garnishes:
Diced white onion, rinsed with cool water
Dried Mexican oregano or marjoram
Chopped ripe Hass avocado
Minced serrano chiles
Lime wedges
Tortilla chips or broken tostadas

Cover the tomatillos with water as needed in a medium pot and simmer over medium heat them until they are soft. Transfer the tomatillos and their cooking water to a blender, along with the pepitas, serrano, and the hoja santa or sorrel leaves (if using) and purée them until smooth. (For the smoothest texture, press the purée through a strainer.)

Dry the pot thoroughly and heat the oil in it over medium-high heat. Add the tomatillo purée to the pot and cook it for 5 minutes, stirring occasionally. Add the 4 cups water, epazote or cilantro, salt, chayote or Mexican gray squash, hominy, and beans, stir, and simmer for 8 to 10 minutes, until the squash is al dente. Serve with any or all of the garnishes.

Chilled Avocado Soup
Sopa Fría de Aguacate

MAKES 4 SERVINGS

This soup is one of the first soups I ever made when I started cooking, but only later did I learn that my creation mirrored what many other cooks in Mexico had already been doing. Some people add raw white onion to the soup, something which I generally don't like, but I've included it as an option in the recipe because it's such a popular addition.

Soup:
2 cups chopped ripe Hass avocado
2 to 4 serrano chiles, seeded and roughly chopped
Juice of 4 limes
1 teaspoon salt
2 1/2 cups water
1/2 medium white onion, coarsely chopped, optional

Garnishes:
1 Roma tomato, seeded and diced
2 small serrano chiles, seeded and minced
1/4 cup minced white onion
2 tablespoons minced fresh cilantro

In a blender or food processor, purée the avocado, serranos, lime juice, salt, water, and onion until smooth. Refrigerate until chilled. To serve, ladle the soup into bowls and garnish with a sprinkle of any or all of the garnishes.

Caldo of Sweet Potato and Chard
Caldo de Camotes y Alcegas

MAKES 6 SERVINGS

This simple soup features a mildly spicy broth married with the earthy sweetness of white sweet potatoes and the lushness of wilted chard. It's not only delicious, it's a powerhouse of nutrition. Chard, sweet potatoes, and beans conspire to fight cancer and regulate blood sugar and are naturally low in fat. That's a win for me.

5 cups water

Corn oil, for frying

4 ancho chiles

10 cloves pan-roasted garlic

1 1/4 teaspoons salt

1 teaspoon dried Mexican oregano

1 medium white sweet potato, chopped into 1-inch pieces

1 bunch chard, greens and stems sliced paper thin

1 1/2 cups cooked pinto beans or 1 (15-ounce) can pinto beans, drained and rinsed

Bring the water to a boil in a medium pot. Heat 1/8 inch of corn oil in a medium skillet over medium heat. Add the anchos and fry them for 20 seconds on each side. Place the anchos in the boiling water, reduce it to a simmer, and simmer the anchos for 6 to 8 minutes. Remove them from the water and when they are cool enough to handle, remove the stems. In a blender or food processor, purée the anchos, garlic, salt, oregano, and the water used to simmer the anchos until smooth. Return the purée to the pot and bring it to a simmer. Add the sweet potato, chard, and beans and cook until the sweet potatoes are al dente, about 6 minutes.

Make It Low-Fat: Skip frying the anchos, omit the oil, and simply rehydrate the anchos in the water.

Lime Soup

Sopa de Lima

MAKES 4 TO 5 SERVINGS

Sopa de lima is a classic Yucatecan soup, but its popularity is certainly not limited to Yucatán. Even before the soup is finished, the aroma of the simmering broth brightens a kitchen with citrus, caramelized onion and garlic, a hint of chile, and lively cinnamon and cloves. I hope once you make it, it will become a popular staple in your kitchen, too. Feel free to try other veggies besides zucchini in the soup. Some of my favorite alternatives include chayotes, carrots, sweet potatoes, and jicama. Finally, sopa de lima and its many variations are traditionally served with fried tortilla chips, but I find that blue corn chips work exceptionally well with this soup and make for a nice presentation while saving the time of cutting and frying tortilla strips.

Broth:

1 medium white onion, cut in half

1 bulb garlic, the top third sliced off

1 banana chile, unseeded, or 1 Anaheim chile, unseeded

6 cups water

Juice of 2 limes

Juice of 1 orange

2 vegetable bouillon cubes

1/3 teaspoon freshly ground black pepper

1 (2-inch) cinnamon stick or 1/4 teaspoon ground cinnamon

Pinch ground cloves

Salt, to taste

Vegetables and Beans:

2 to 3 tablespoons olive oil or Garlic-Citrus Olive Oil (page 43)

1 medium white onion, cut into 1/2-inch dice

3 Roma tomatoes, cut into 1-inch pieces

1 poblano chile, coarsely chopped

2 medium zucchini, chopped into 1/2-inch pieces

1 1/2 cups cooked pinto beans or 1 (15-ounce) can pinto beans, drained and
   rinsed

Garnishes:

1 orange, sliced paper thin

1 lime, sliced paper thin

Chopped fresh cilantro, to taste

Blue corn chips

Place both halves of the onion, the garlic (cut-side down), and the banana chile or Anaheim chile in a 3-quart pot over medium heat. Cover the pot. After 5 minutes, flip the chile and then re-cover the pot, letting everything roast for 5 more minutes. Add the water, lime juice, orange juice, bouillon cubes, pepper, cinnamon stick or ground cinnamon, cloves, and salt and bring the broth to a simmer. Cover, reduce the heat to medium-low, and simmer the broth for 30 minutes. Remove the onion, garlic bulb, banana or Anaheim chile, and cinnamon stick (if using), but keep the broth simmering.

Heat the olive oil or Garlic-Citrus Olive Oil in a sauté pan at just above medium heat. Add the onion, tomatoes, and poblano and sauté for 7 to 8 minutes. Add the sautéed onion mixture to the pot of broth, along with the zucchinis and beans. Simmer for 5 to 6 minutes, until the zucchinis soften. To serve, ladel the soup into bowls and garnish earch serving with a slice of orange, a couple slices of lime, fresh cilantro, and corn chips.

Tomato Black Bean Soup
Sopa Tarasca

MAKES 6 SERVINGS

This soup, named after the Tarascos people of Michoacán, is a soulful blend of black beans, onions, garlic, tomatoes, and chiles. Like many of the best Mexican soups, it's comfort food that can easily be upgraded if you like. I like to serve mine in a bowl-size cazuela to accentuate the rustic, homey feel of the soup. If you want to kick up the heat, add a small handful of chiles de árbol to the mix.

Soup:
3 Roma tomatoes, coarsely chopped
1 ancho chile, stemmed and seeded
1 1/2 cups water
3 cloves garlic
1/2 medium white onion, coarsely chopped
1 to 2 tablespoons corn oil
4 cups cooked black beans, puréed
2 1/2 cups vegetable broth
1 teaspoon salt

Garnishes:
Fried ancho chile strips
Tortilla chips or strips
Chopped ripe Hass avocado
Vegan sour cream, whipped vigorously

In a 3-quart pot, combine the tomatoes, ancho, and water and simmer over medium heat for about 10 minutes. Transfer the tomatoes, ancho, and water to a blender and wipe out the pot. Add the garlic and onion the blender and purée until smooth. (Press the purée through a strainer if you want it completely smooth.)

Add the oil to the pot and heat it over medium-high heat. Add the purée and cook for about 5 minutes, slowly stirring. Reduce the heat to medium and add the puréed beans, vegetable broth, and salt. Simmer the soup for 10 minutes. Add liquid if necessary to ensure the soup is creamy but not incredibly thick. Serve with any or all of the garnishes.

A Bean Soup Caution

There are quite a few bean soups in Mexican cuisine. You'll want to take particular care not to burn them. Beans are starchy and easily stick to the bottom of a pot, and charred beans are not a desirable flavor. Bean soups, however, are awesome.

Chayotes in Mole Poblano
(page 176)

MAIN DISHES

Platos

This chapter contains main dish recipes for breakfast, second breakfast, lunch, dinner, and second dinner. If that sounds like it's a chapter for hobbits, you wouldn't be too far off. Mexicans love food, and there are several opportunities throughout the day for a good meal.

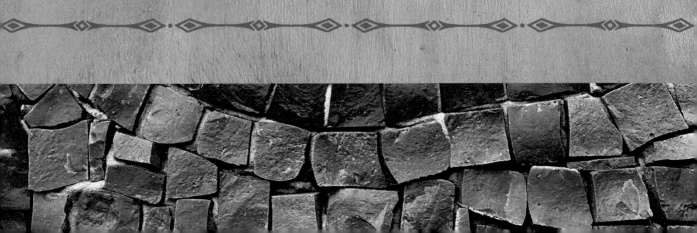

The first meal of the day is desayuno, an early morning breakfast that consists of a drink and perhaps a pastry or fruit. It's the kick start to the morning. From around nine to noon is almeurzo, which is a heavier breakfast or brunch meals, and this is where a lot of Mexican breakfasts differ from what we see in the States, because almuerzo can consist of chilaquiles, tacos, enchiladas, tamales, and other dishes we normally think of as dinner dishes. Personally, I prefer an enchilada for breakfast rather than a bowl of oatmeal. The main meal of the day is the comida, taken around midafternoon, which often features a thick stew called a guisado, a soup, a salad, and a sweet treat. The final meal of the day, the late-night meal, is called cena and can be something light like a few tortillas or street tacos or a more formal dinner on the town with friends. In between those meals are opportunities to buy antojitos from all the street stalls. It's no wonder Mexico is one of the dining capitals of the world.

Most of the dishes in this section are meant to be served with a salad or soup, tortillas, and a side of beans, but don't feel like you have to go through all that effort for one meal. I'm a fan of one-dish meals and I typically only make one of these dishes and forgo the rest, unless I happen to have beans, tortillas, or the ingredients for a very quick and easy salad in the refrigerator.

Some of the recipes are complex and require a time commitment while others are simple to put together. While several of them are traditionally breakfast recipes, I've included them in this general main dish section simply because many traditional Mexican breakfasts would be considered lunch or dinner plates elsewhere.

Pasta Baked in Chipotle Tomato Sauce
Sopa Seca

MAKES 2 SERVINGS

You may think you're getting a soup by the name ("sopa" means "soup"), but this is actually a pasta dish baked in sauce until the noodles have almost completely absorbed the sauce. That's where the "seca" comes in, because the name sopa seca actually translates to "dry soup." It's Mexican comfort food at its finest: warming, homey, stick-to-your ribs comfortable with a little heat to give it some extra oomph. You can make this with roasted tomatillos instead of tomatoes if you want a tangy version of this delicious dish. Fideo pasta is often sold at Mexican markets cut into pieces specifically for this recipe.

- 3 Roma tomatoes, pan-roasted
- 2 chipotles in adobo
- 2 cloves garlic
- 1/4 small white onion, finely chopped
- 1 cup water
- 1/2 teaspoon salt
- 2 tablespoons olive oil
- 4 ounces fideo or vermicelli noodles, broken into 2- to 4-inch pieces
- 1/4 cup Simple Queso Fresco (page 42) or crumbly vegan cheese of your choice
- 2 tablespoons minced fresh cilantro

Preheat the oven to 350°F. Lightly oil a small baking dish and set aside. In a blender or food processor, purée the tomatoes, chipotles, garlic, onion, water, and salt and set aside.

Heat the oil in a medium skillet over medium heat. Add the pasta and toast it about 4 minutes. As soon as it is golden brown (it's especially important that the pasta does not become dark brown), add the sauce and quickly stir. Transfer the pasta to the baking dish and bake for 10 minutes.

To serve, transfer the pasta to plates and garnish with the Simple Queso Fresco and cilantro.

The Smallest Batch of Sauce

It's hard to make a smaller batch of sauce than this because of the small quantities used, so if you're only making this for one or two people, you'll have plenty of sauce left over. That's not necessarily a bad thing!

Chilaquiles Two Ways

Commonly eaten for breakfast (or a late-night snack), chilaquiles are corn chips or broken tostada shells smothered in chile sauce and topped with a variety of ingredients. They are a great way to use up yesterday's tortillas or chips, and the thicker chips work best with these recipes. Eggs dominate the Mexican breakfast, so I've prepared my breakfast version with a tofu scramble. Think of it as tofu ranchera on corn chips drowned in chile sauce. Yum! The chilaquile that I eat as a late-night snack employs a green sauce and is topped with beans and jackfruit or shredded seitan. You can make the sauces yourself or you can use a jar of good-quality salsa in place of the sauces. Each recipe makes 1 chilaquile.

Breakfast Chilaquile
Chilaquiles para Desayuno

4 ounces extra-firm tofu, drained and crumbled

1/8 teaspoon ground turmeric

1/8 teaspoon salt (preferably Indian black salt)

1 cup Basic Guajillo Chile Sauce (page 43) or red salsa of your choice

2 cups corn chips

1/4 cup cooked pinto beans, rinsed

1/2 ripe Hass avocado, pitted, peeled, and coarsely chopped

1 tablespoon minced red onion, optional

In a small skillet over medium heat, mix together the tofu, turmeric, and salt and cook for about 5 minutes. Remove the tofu scramble from the skillet and set aside. Add the Basic Guajillo Chile Sauce to the skillet and warm it over medium heat for 3 to 4 minutes. Pile the chips on a plate, pour the sauce over them, and make sure they are all well coated. Top the chips with the tofu scramble, beans, avocado, and onion (if using). Serve immediately, before the chips become too soggy.

Late-Night Snack Chilaquile
Antojitos de Chilaquiles

1 tablespoon corn or olive oil

1/2 cup shredded water-packed canned jackfruit or shredded seitan or
   meatless strips

1/8 teaspoon salt

1 teaspoon chile powder

2 cups corn chips

1 cup Salsa Verde (page 50)

1/2 ripe Hass avocado, pitted, peeled, and coarsely chopped or cut into 1/4-
   inch thick slices

Heat the oil in a small skillet over medium heat. Add the jackfruit and sauté for 5 minutes. Add the salt and chile powder, stir the jackfruit a couple times, and remove it from the heat. Pile the chips on a plate, pour the Salsa Verde over them, making sure they are well coated, and top with the sautéed jackfruit and avocado.

Red Chile–Marinated Tempeh
Tempeh Adobada

MAKES 4 CUPS

Tempeh's nutty flavor and hearty texture are the perfect companions for this incredible red chile marinade. Whether you grill it or roast it, you are in for a lively treat. Make extra, because you'll probably want leftovers! Serve with corn tortillas or rice, chopped avocado, sliced red onions or grilled cebollitas, and lime wedges. For a truly exceptional flavor, smoke the marinated tempeh with mesquite wood in a smoker for 6 to 8 hours, then finish it off on the grill.

    1 to 2 tablespoons corn oil
    6 ancho chiles, seeded and stemmed
    Boiling water (reserve 1 1/2 cups after the chiles are rehydrated)
    1 to 2 dried chipotles, optional
    3 cloves garlic
    1/4 cup apple cider vinegar
    1 teaspoon dried oregano
    3/4 teaspoon freshly ground black pepper
    1/3 teaspoon ground cumin
    1/8 teaspoon ground cloves
    1/8 teaspoon ground cinnamon
    1 teaspoon dried Mexican oregano
    1 teaspoon grated piloncillo or turbinado sugar
    32 ounces tempeh, cut into 4 x 1-inch strips

Heat the oil in a medium skillet over medium heat. Add the anchos and fry them for 10 to 30 seconds per side (do not burn them). Transfer the anchos to a heat-resistant bowl. Add the chipotles to the bowl (if using). Pour the boiling water over the chiles and let them rehydrate for 10 to 15 minutes, until soft. Reserve 1 1/2 cups of the chile water and discard the rest. In a blender, combine the anchos, chipotles, reserved chile water, garlic, apple cider vinegar, oregano, pepper, cumin, cloves, cinnamon, oregano, and piloncillo or sugar. Purée until smooth. For a smoother sauce, press the mixture through a fine-mesh strainer. Place the tempeh in a medium bowl, add the sauce, and gently toss. You can cook the tempeh right away, but it will achieve maximum flavor if you let it marinate overnight in the refrigerator.

In the Oven: Preheat the oven to 300°F. Line a 9-inch baking dish with parchment paper and spread 2 table-spoons olive oil on it. Add the marinated tempeh and bake, uncovered, for 1 hour.

On the Grill: Bring the grill to medium heat and spray the rack with oil. Add the tempeh and grill until it is lightly charred on all sides. The time will vary based on the exact heat of your grill and how far the rack is from the fire, about 6 to 8 minutes per side. You'll lose much of the sauce on the grill, so reserve some from the bowl to use as a salsa.

Variations: Use sliced portobello mushrooms, sliced eggplant, or meatless strips instead of tempeh, following the recipe the same way.

Tofu and Tortillas in Red Salsa
Tofu Rancheras

MAKES 4 SERVINGS

This is about one of the easiest breakfasts you can make. Lightly fry a couple corn tortillas, make a tofu scramble, and either use your favorite red salsa or use Pico de Gallo. That's it. If you have a premade salsa, this recipe might take you 10 minutes. You can even skip frying the tortillas and use tostada shells or bake the tortillas instead. I usually serve these two tortillas to a plate.

Corn oil, for frying
4 (5- to 6-inch) corn tortillas
8 ounces extra-firm tofu, drained and crumbled
3/4 teaspoon ground turmeric
3/4 teaspoon Indian black salt, smoked salt, or sea salt
1 cup Pico de Gallo (page 47) or store-bought red salsa
1 ripe Hass avocado, pitted, peeled, and cut into 1/4-inch slices
2 tablespoons chopped fresh cilantro

Add 1/8 inch of oil to a medium skillet and bring it to a medium-high heat. Add the tortillas one at a time and fry them for 15 seconds per side, so that they are lightly toasted and immediately transfer them to a plate. Reduce the heat to medium and add the tofu, turmeric, and salt. Heat the tofu until it is warm and set aside. Smother the tortillas with the salsa, then top with the tofu scramble, avocado, and cilantro.

Mexican Meatballs in Serrano Tomato Sauce
Albóndigas en Salsa Ranchera

MAKES 3 SERVINGS

I find albóndigas, the quintessential Mexican meatball, fascinating. The word itself is a derivative of the Arabic word "al-búnduqa," meaning "hazelnut" or "a small ball." They're the perfect example of how a Middle Eastern food was transformed by the journey to Spain and then to Mexico, where it was adapted to the regional cuisine. What really sets these meatballs apart for me is the use of pasilla chiles and fresh mint. This inventive use of ingredients gives albóndigas their full-bodied, complex taste full of high notes and soul-satisfying flavors. Serve these over rice with fresh corn tortillas and beans and garnish with fresh mint.

Albóndigas:
3 cloves garlic, minced

8 to 10 fresh mint leaves, minced

1 teaspoon salt

1/2 teaspoon freshly ground black pepper

1 tablespoon chile powder of your choice

1/4 cup mashed black beans

1/3 cup cooked long-grain brown rice

1/2 small white onion, minced and rinsed with cool water

2 cups ground tempeh or seitan

Corn oil or olive oil, for brushing

Salsa Ranchera:
5 Roma tomatoes

1/2 small white onion, coarsely chopped

3 cloves garlic

1 to 2 serrano chiles, stemmed

1/2 teaspoon salt

Juice of 1 lime

2 tablespoons corn or olive oil

Preheat the oven to 400°F. Line a baking sheet with parchment paper or a silicone mat and set it aside. Smash the garlic, mint, salt, and pepper together, preferably using a mortar and pestle or the flat side of a large knife. In a small mixing bowl, combine the garlic mixture and chile powder with the mashed black beans until thoroughly incorporated. Add the rice, onion, and tempeh or seitan into the bean mixture. Shape the bean mixture into 1-inch balls. Arrange them on the prepared baking sheet and lightly brush them with the oil. Bake the meatballs for 20 minutes.

While the meatballs are baking, place the tomatoes in a dry medium skillet, preferably cast iron, over medium heat and cook them until they blister. Rotate them until the skin has blackened and split on all sides.

Transfer the tomatoes to a blender and purée them along with the onion, garlic, serranos, salt, and lime juice. Heat the oil in a large skillet over medium-high heat. Add the sauce and cook it for 8 to 10 minutes, slowly scraping the bottom of the skillet. Remove the sauce from the heat. Add the meatballs to the sauce and gently toss to coat them. Serve hot.

Mushroom Chilorio
Chilorio de Hongos

MAKES 4 CUPS

It's hard to think about the open-air markets of Sinaloa without thinking about chilorio, but while I love the chile and spice sauce, traditional chilorio has not been a compassionate dish—until now. Dried mushrooms take the place of shredded pork in my version of this incredible stew, both for texture and for their umami flavor. Don't use expensive dried wild mushrooms. They won't make a difference except in your pocket book. Use dried sliced button or shiitake mushrooms, which can often be purchased in bulk at many Asian markets. Chilorio is incredibly versatile. Use it on its own or as a filling for tacos, burritos, empanadas, sopes, tamales, and more.

 4 ancho chiles, stemmed and seeded
 8 cloves garlic
 1 teaspoon dried Mexican oregano
 3/4 teaspoon ground cumin
 1/2 teaspoon freshly ground black pepper
 3/4 teaspoon salt
 1/4 cup distilled white vinegar
 3 tablespoons vegan shortening, optional
 4 cups dried sliced mushrooms

Toast the anchos, then rehydrate them for 15 minutes in a bowl with enough hot water to cover them. Drain the anchos and transfer them to a blender. Add the garlic, oregano, cumin, pepper, salt, and vinegar and purée until smooth.

Fried-Sauce Version: If you are using the shortening to fry the sauce, bring the shortening to just above medium heat in a wide, deep pan. Add the sauce and fry it for 15 to 20 minutes, stirring it every minute or so. Add the mushrooms and once they have absorbed the sauce, remove the chilorio from the heat and serve.

Unfried-Sauce Version: Transfer the sauce to a 2-quart pot and simmer it over medium heat for 15 to 20 minutes. Add the mushrooms and once they have absorbed the sauce, remove the chilorio from the heat and serve.

Tortillas Smothered in Bean Sauce
Enfrijoladas

MAKES 5 SERVINGS

Enfrijoladas—tortillas enrobed in a rich, luscious bean sauce—are a favorite Oaxacan breakfast. I like to garnish mine with fresh tomato, onion, avocado, and some pepitas for added crunch. They're often served with crema, as well, but I find the avocado adds enough creaminess. They only take a few minutes to make, but they'll leave you feeling satisfied for hours. Although they are supposed to be eaten for breakfast, I do not discriminate. I will eat enfrijoladas any time of the day! The sauce is often made with toasted avocado leaves, which are often available at Mexican markets, but if you can't get an avocado leaf, don't worry. Simply omit it.

- 1 avocado leaf, optional
- 2 teaspoons corn oil
- 1/2 medium white onion, finely chopped
- 1 3/4 cups cooked black beans
- 1 chipotle in abodo
- Water, as needed
- Salt, to taste
- 5 thick (5 to 6-inch) homemade corn tortillas or 10 (5 to 6-inch) store-bought corn tortillas

Garnishes:
- 2 Roma tomatoes, cut into 1/2-inch dice
- 1/4 medium white onion, cut into 1/4-inch dice
- 1 to 2 ripe Hass avocados, pitted, peeled, and coarsely chopped
- 1/4 cup salted toasted pepitas

Toast the avocado leaf (if using) in a dry medium skillet over medium heat for a few seconds per side and transfer it to a blender. Return the skillet to medium heat. Add the oil and onion to the skillet and sauté the onion until it is lightly browned, 7 to 8 minutes. Transfer the onion to the blender, along with the beans and chipotle. Purée the onion mixture until smooth and add enough water to create a creamy, soupy consistency. Add salt to taste. Transfer the sauce back to the skillet and leave it on the heat just long enough to warm it throughout.

Dip the tortillas in the sauce. If you are using store-bought tortillas, they'll be a little thin, so make a stack of 2 dipped tortillas per serving. Pour any extra sauce over the tortillas. Garnish with tomato, onion, avocado, and pepitas.

Mushroom Crêpes in Poblano Chile Sauce
Crêpes de Champinones en Salsa de Chile Poblano

MAKES 8 CRÊPES

Wow, crêpes and chiles—two of my favorite foods in one meal! This dish is quintessential Mexican-French fusion. It's a sauce of roasted poblano chiles and a classic béchamel sauce poured over a crêpe filled with mushrooms, corn, and onion. The recipe dates from the mid-1800s, first made for the court of Emperor Maximilian, the Austrian emperor of Mexico. Traditionally served at weddings in Mexico City, it's usually made with huitlacoche and squash blossoms, both delicacies, but not always easy to get north of the border where squash blossoms are highly seasonal. My version uses cremini mushrooms instead of huitlacoche and omits the squash blossoms, making it an any-time-of-the-year recipe.

Sauce:

3 tablespoons vegan butter or olive oil

3 tablespoons flour

1/2 cup water

3 roasted poblano chiles, peeled and seeded

1/4 cup slivered almonds

3/4 teaspoon salt

1/4 teaspoon grated nutmeg

Filling:

1 tablespoon vegan butter or olive oil

1 large white onion, cut into 1/4-inch pieces

2 cloves garlic, minced

20 cremini mushrooms, lightly rinsed, patted dry, and quartered

1/4 teaspoon salt

1/2 teaspoon freshly ground black pepper

1 cup fresh or thawed frozen corn kernels

1/2 teaspoon chipotle chile flakes, optional

Crêpes:

1 cup plain unsweetened almond milk

1/4 cup melted vegan butter or olive oil, plus more for cooking

2 tablespoons agave syrup

1 cup unbleached all-purpose flour or whole-wheat pastry flour

1/3 teaspoon salt

2 tablespoons pine nuts, optional

Sauce: Heat the butter or oil in a medium skillet over medium heat. Add the flour and stir, cooking until the flour turns a light brown color, about 5 to 6 minutes. Slowly add the water, stirring constantly, to avoid lumps. Keep the flour mixture on the heat. In a blender or food processor, purée the poblanos, almonds, salt, and nutmeg until completely smooth. Add the purée to the skillet, stir to combine, and cook for 5 minutes. Set aside.

Filling: Heat the butter or oil in a large skillet over medium heat. Add the onion and sauté until the onion is soft and translucent, about 4 to 5 minutes. Add the garlic and sauté 1 minute. Add the mushrooms, salt, and pepper, and cook, about 10 minutes, until the mushrooms have reduced to about half their original size. Add the corn and chipotle flakes (if using), stir, and set aside.

Crêpes: Combine the almond milk, melted butter or oil, and agave syrup in a medium mixing bowl. Add the flour and salt and stir until you have a thin batter. Heat a crêpe pan or small skillet over medium-high heat. Add enough butter or oil to barely coat the pan. Add 1/4 cup of the batter and quickly swirl it until it coats the bottom of the pan. Cook the crêpe for 1 minute, then flip and cook for 30 seconds. Gently remove it from the pan and repeat this process until all the crêpes are cooked.

To Assemble: Divide the filling evenly among all the crêpes and fold them over. Transfer them to serving plates and liberally pour the sauce over the crêpes. Garnish with the optional pine nuts if you want to add some crunch to the dish.

To Make the Traditional Filling

If you want to make the traditional version of this recipe, substitute 2 1/2 cups huitlacoche for the mushrooms and cook for 5 minutes. Once the huitlacoche is cooked, add 10 chopped squash blossoms to the pan and cook until they are just softened. Add the corn, remove from the heat, and the filling is done. Now you've got traditional chilango wedding crêpes!

Pasta and Trumpet Mushrooms in Chile-Apricot Sauce

Pasta de Hongos en Salsa de Chiles y Albaricoques

MAKES 4 SERVINGS

The sauce for this dish is based on an apricot-chile dip called chamoy that is eaten all over Mexico. This sauce is not exactly a chamoy, because it's chile-heavy, but that tweak turned this into the perfect sauce for a main dish. Not too sweet, not too spicy, but with a complexity and depth that dances along the tongue, revealing something new with every bite. I get hungry just writing about this sauce, let alone making it. I strongly suggest making a double or triple batch of the sauce and refrigerating the leftover for use with other dishes or even using it as the base for a soup. If you want to make the more traditional chamoy sauce, cut the amount of chiles in half and add 1/4 cup of sugar.

Sauce:
1/4 cup olive oil
2 ancho chiles, stemmed
2 guajillo chiles, stemmed
1 chipotle in adobo
1/4 cup dried apricots
Juice of 1 lime
2 cups reserved chile water
1 teaspoon salt

Fettuccine and Mushrooms:
8 ounces fettuccine, broken in half
4 king trumpet mushrooms, lightly rinsed, patted dry, and sliced into 1/4-
    inch thick discs or 1 1/2 cups chopped wild mushrooms
4 cloves garlic, minced
1/4 teaspoon salt

Garnishes:
4 dried apricots, sliced into 1/4-inch thick pieces
2 tablespoons chopped fresh mint
1/4 cup salted toasted pepitas

Bring about 4 cups hot water to a boil in a 2-quart pot over medium-high heat and keep it boiling while you complete the next step. Heat the oil in a large skillet over medium heat. Fry the anchos and guajillos in the oil for 15 to 20 seconds per side, then immediately transfer them to a bowl that can withstand the boiling water. Leave the oil in the skillet. Pour the boiling water over the anchos and guajillos and let them sit for 15 minutes.

In a blender or food processor, purée the anchos, guajillos, chipotle, apricots, lime juice, chile water, and salt. Set this sauce aside.

Boil the fettuccini and drain it, but do not rinse it. While the fettuccine is boiling, sauté the king trumpet or wild mushrooms for 7 to 8 minutes over medium heat in the same skillet and oil used to fry the chiles. Add the garlic and salt and sauté 2 more minutes. Add the sauce to the skillet and simmer for 3 minutes. Add the fettuccine to the skillet, toss, and immediately transfer to a serving dish. Garnish with the sliced apricots, mint, and pepitas.

Chayotes in Mole Poblano
Chayote en Mole Poblano

MAKES 6 SERVINGS

Mole Poblano, the most famous of Mexican sauces, is a heady mix of chiles, nuts, spices, bread, and several sweet items. One story that tells of its origin claims that the nuns of the Convent of Santa Rosa in Puebla panicked when they heard the archbishop was coming to visit because they had nothing adequate to serve. An angel came and gave them the secret to mole Poblano. After hours of preparing their mole, they finally had a sauce that won over the heart of the archbishop. Regardless of its origin, mole Poblano became a national dish associated with festivals, weddings, and other important events. Making mole Poblano from scratch takes a time commitment (which is one reason it's a special celebratory food and not an everyday food), but it is well worth the effort. I often make triple batches and freeze the remainder so that I can have mole for weeks to come with little effort. When I do make it, I either invite friends over to help make it and turn it into a party (I highly suggest this!), or I make it alone and let the process become a soulful, tasty meditation.

Chayote and Beans:

3 large chayotes, cut in half

Garlic-Citrus Olive Oil (page 43) or olive oil

1/2 teaspoon coarse sea salt

2 cups cooked Colorado or pinto beans, rinsed

Mole Poblano:

2 teaspoons chile seeds (ancho, guajillo, or mulato)

1/4 teaspoon coriander seeds

4 cloves or 1/8 teaspoon ground cloves

3 black peppercorns or 1/8 teaspoon freshly ground black pepper

1/8 teaspoon anise seeds or pinch ground anise

1 (1/2-inch) Mexican cinnamon stick or 1/3 teaspoon ground cinnamon

2 tablespoons sesame seeds

1/2 cup corn oil, divided

1/4 cup slivered almonds

1/4 cup raw pepitas

1/3 cup golden raisins

1 (5-inch) corn tortilla

2 (1/2-inch thick) French baguette slices

1 small ripe plantain, peeled and coarsely chopped

1/2 medium white onion, coarsely chopped

3 ancho chiles, stemmed

4 pasilla or additional ancho chiles, stemmed

4 mulato chiles, stemmed

Boiling water, as needed

2 Roma tomatoes, pan-roasted

3 cloves garlic, pan-roasted
1 (1-ounce) wedge Mexican chocolate
1 (1-ounce) piece piloncillo or 1 tablespoon turbinado sugar
Salt, to taste

Brush the chayotes with the Garlic-Citrus Olive Oil. Toss with the salt. Either grill the chayotes until they are heavily browned on both sides or roast them in the oven at 450°F for 20 minutes. Chop the chayotes into 1-inch pieces and set aside.

In an iron skillet or heavy-bottomed skillet over medium heat, toast the following individually, stirring slowly: the chile seeds until they are blackened, about 2 minutes; the coriander seeds for 1 minute; the cloves for 1 minute; the peppercorns for 30 seconds; the anise seeds for 30 seconds; the Mexican cinnamon stick for 1 minute; and the sesame seeds for 1 minute. Remove each from the heat and grind into powder. Transfer each to a blender and set aside.

Add 1/4 cup of the corn oil to the skillet. Working one at a time, fry the following individually: the almonds until they are browned, about 2 minutes; the pepitas until they are browned, about 1 1/2 minutes; the raisins until they plump, about 1 1/2 minutes; the tortilla until it is golden, about 1 minute; the French baguette slices until they are golden, about 2 minutes; the plantain until it is browned, about 3 minutes; and the onion until it is browned, about 5 minutes. Transfer each to the blender as you finish each one.

Add the remaining 1/4 cup oil to the skillet over medium heat. Working in batches, fry the anchos, pasillas or additional anchos, and mulatos for 30 seconds, taking care not to burn them. Transfer the chiles to a heat-resistant bowl and pour boiling water over them. Leave the oil in the skillet, but turn the heat off. Wait 20 to 30 minutes for the chiles to rehydrate, then transfer them to the blender along with the tomatoes and garlic. Reserve the chile water.

Purée the spice mixture, slivered almond mixture, and chile mixture, adding enough of the reserved chile water as you blend to create a smooth sauce. Press through a fine-mesh strainer, if you like, for the smoothest sauce. Bring the oil in the skillet to medium-low heat. Add the sauce, Mexican chocolate, piloncillo or turbinado, and salt to the skillet. Slowly simmer this for at least 40 minutes, until oil pools on top of the mole. As the mole thickens, add just enough of the reserved chile water to keep it from sticking to the skillet. If you have the time, you can reduce the heat to low and simmer it for 1 to 2 hours. The longer, the better. Add the chayotes and beans to the mole and serve with rice.

Simplify Your Mole Poblano

You can simplify your mole by using ground spices and not toasting them. You can also skip frying the pepitas and almonds by purchasing them pre-salted and roasted. Time can be saved by not frying the chiles, raisins, onion, and plantain. Simply purée all the ingredients, then add to the skillet. Your mole won't be as rich-tasting, but you'll save a lot of time. Another time-saver is using store-bought mole poblano. I recommend Doña Maria brand jarred mole because it's vegan and commonly available at Mexican markets and many supermarkets. To use it, combine 1 cup of the jarred mole with enough water to make a thick sauce and puree it with 1/2 of a caramelized chopped white onion.

Yellow Mole
Mole Amarillo

MAKES 4 TO 5 SERVINGS

Moles have a reputation for being complex, but that's not always the case. Enter mole amarillo, one of my favorite go-to recipes when I want to showcase great Mexican food to guests and not spend hours in the kitchen. It gets its color from the mix of tomatoes, tomatillos, and chiles, and it's actually more orange than yellow. Traditionally, it's made with chilcostle chiles, a specialty chile grown in Oaxaca that has a moderately hot and unique flavor, but guajillo chiles make a fine substitute. It also uses hoja santa, an herb common in Mexico, but just now showing up in U.S. Mexican markets. If you don't have hoja santa, you can simply omit it.

Mole Amarillo:
2 cloves
2 allspice berries
2 black peppercorns
1/8 teaspoon whole cumin seeds
1 Roma tomato
1 large tomatillo
3 cups water, divided, plus more as needed
2 chilcostle or guajillo chiles, toasted and rehydrated
1 ancho chile, toasted and rehydrated
1/2 small white onion, coarsely chopped
4 cloves garlic
3/4 teaspoon salt
1 tablespoon corn oil
1/4 cup masa harina mixed with 1 cup water
1 hoja santa leaf, sliced paper thin, optional

Vegetables:
2 medium Yukon gold potatoes, chopped into 1-inch pieces
1 medium chayote, chopped into 1-inch pieces
3 cups green beans, trimmed

Combine the cloves, allspice berries, peppercorns, and cumin seeds in a medium skillet and toast them over medium heat for 1 minute. Remove them from the heat and grind them. Simmer the tomato and tomatillo in 1 cup of the water in a small pot over medium heat for 5 minutes. Add the spice mixture, chilcostles or guajillos, ancho, tomato, tomatillo, leftover water, onion, garlic, and salt to a blender and purée until smooth.

Heat the oil in a deep skillet or cazuela over medium heat. Add the purée and fry, stirring, for 5 minutes. Add the masa harina and water mixture and simmer until thickened. Add the remaining 2 cups water and stir until combined. Add the potatoes, chayote, and green beans and simmer until the potatoes are al dente, about 7 minutes. Add the hoja santa during the last minute, if using. Remove from the heat and serve.

Potatoes and Chorizo
Papas y Chorizo

MAKES 2 SERVINGS

An easy dish to put together if you have premade vegan chorizo, this can be eaten on its own, used as a taco filling, a topping for chilaquiles, a burrito filling, an enchilada filling, or mixed with a tofu scramble for breakfast.

2 teaspoons olive oil or Garlic-Citrus Olive Oil (page 43)
2 medium Yukon gold potatoes, cut into 1/2-inch dice
1/4 cup water
1/3 teaspoon salt
1/2 cup Red Chorizo (page 40) or store-bought vegan chorizo
1 poblano chile, roasted, peeled, seeded, and chopped

Heat the oil in a medium skillet over medium heat. Add the potatoes and cook until they start to brown, about 7 minutes. Turn the heat up to medium-high and add the water and salt. Cook until the water evaporates. Reduce the heat to medium. Add the Red Chorizo and poblano and heat until warmed throughout.

Fish-Free Bacalao
MAKES ABOUT 3 SERVINGS

Bacalao is a thick fish stew that you can easily veganize using vegan fish fillets or oyster mushrooms.

Olive and Tomato Salsa (page 53)
1/3 cup water
2 medium Yukon gold potatoes, cut into 1/2-inch dice
2 dried bay leaves
1 cup sliced vegan fish fillets or chopped fresh oyster mushrooms

Bring the Olive and Tomato Salsa to a simmer in a medium saucepan over medium heat, then add the water, potatoes, bay leaves, and vegan fish fillets or oyster mushrooms and simmer for 10 minutes. Remove and discard the bay leaves before serving. Serve hot.

GRILLED FARE

Asadas

◇

Grilled and smoked foods are an integral part of Mexican cuisine, from simple ingredients like grilled chiles and grilled cebollitas (large Mexican spring onions) to seared cactus paddles, fire-roasted salsas, and smoked chorizo.

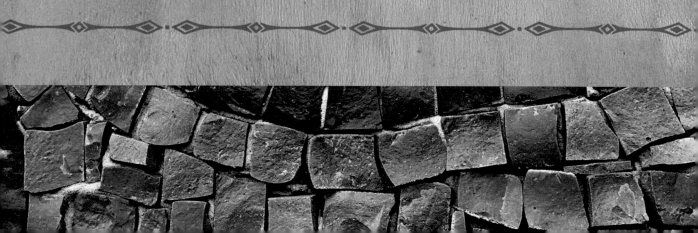

There is an entire category of tacos dedicated just to the grill—you can't do anything al carbon without an open flame. For best effect, you'll want a charcoal or wood-fire grill. The wood and open flame don't just create flavor from the smoke—the fire dancing around the wood creates small, uneven cooking patterns that add complexity to a dish in a way that the perfectly even flame of a gas grill can't. Aside from that, I find the movement of the flames and wood meditative and intriguing at the same time. The most common wood used throughout Central and Northern Mexico is mesquite wood, though you will certainly find other woods used like orange wood, apple wood, alder wood, and even eucalyptus. If you have a gas grill, you can still get great smoky flavor into your meals (with or without a smoker attachment) by using mesquite wood chips that have been soaked in water for 30 minutes.

For ingredients that you want seared, bring the flames as close to the grill rack as possible. These foods cook quickly and develop some charring. For foods for which you want a smokier flavor, keep the flame low from the grill rack. Make sure these ingredients stay hydrated either with liquid or oil, since they will be on the fire for a longer period of time. You can also control how quickly your ingredients cook, and thereby how much smoke and char they acquire, by their horizontal distance from the flames. The farther away from the flames you place your food, the longer they cook.

You can impart a distinct flavor to these longer-cooking ingredients by wrapping them in different leaves. In the States, foil is the item I see used most often (and foil definitely has a flavor, though I'm not sure it's one you want), but you can wrap ingredients in banana leaves, fresh corn husks, hoja santa leaves, and even nestle them inside a large split chile.

If you have a dedicated smoker, I'm assuming you already know how to smoke. If you don't have a dedicated smoker, you can still smoke your food for several hours. Let the coals or wood die down to a low heat, then move them to one side of your grill. Place your ingredients to smoke on the other side of the grill and close the lid. Make sure to keep your ingredients hydrated. The less you open the grill lid, the better. About 2 hours of smoke time will get you a good (but not overwhelming) smoke flavor for most foods. If you want your food particularly smoky, which is often the case when that ingredient has to compete against lots of other bold flavors, then leave your food to smoke on the grill for 4 to 6 hours. Using the grill in this manner is an excellent way to make your own dried smoked chiles, like chipotles. I love making smoked chorizo, smoked mushrooms, smoked chiles, smoked tempeh, and smoked seitan.

If you don't have a grill, but you still want smoked ingredients, you can use a smoking bag. These are foil bags with pockets in the foil that contain tiny wood chips that smoke when you place them in the oven.

Chile Rub for Grilled Vegetables
Recado para Verduras Asadas

MAKES 1/4 CUP

There are lots of rubs and marinades you can use on the grill, but this one is my go-to staple. It's versatile, and you can easily modify it to create different flavors. I make a couple batches of this at a time, then jar it so I've got it readily available. It also makes a great general chile powder you can use in other recipes.

2 guajillo chiles

4 chiles de árbol or 1/2 teaspoon chipotle powder, optional

1 teaspoon dried Mexican oregano

1/4 teaspoon freshly ground black pepper

1/4 teaspoon ground cumin

Pinch ground cinnamon

1/2 teaspoon salt

Optional Additions:

1/4 teaspoon achiote powder

1/2 teaspoon garlic powder

1 teaspoon cocoa powder

1 teaspoon ground coffee

1 teaspoon lime or orange zest

Grind the guajillos in a blender or spice grinder If you want a hot chile rub, grind the chiles de árbol or use chipotle powder. Combine the ground guajillos, chiles de árbol or chipotle powder (if using), oregano, pepper, cumin, cinnamon, and salt in a small mixing bowl. Add any or all of the optional additions to create variations on the chile rub. Keep in a spice jar or airtight container and the mix will last for a month.

Grilled Portobellos
in Serrano-Cilantro Sauce
Portobello Asada en Salsa de Chile Serrano y Cilantro

MAKES 2 SERVINGS

This is a super-easy grilled filling that you can use to make tacos, quesadillas, or simply eat as is. Most of your time will be spent warming up your grill!

Serrano-Cilantro Sauce:
2 to 4 serrano chiles, seeded
2 cups coarsely chopped fresh cilantro
3 cloves garlic
1/2 teaspoon salt
3 tablespoons white vinegar (any kind)
2 tablespoons olive oil

Portobellos:
2 large portobello mushrooms, lightly rinsed and patted dry
2 tablespoons olive oil
1/2 teaspoon freshly ground black pepper
1/2 teaspoon salt

Accompaniments:
Corn tortillas
Pickled Onions (page 39)

Sauce: In a blender, combine the serranos, cilantro, garlic, salt, vinegar, and oil, and purée until mostly smooth. Set aside.

Portobellos: Light the grill and let the heat reach about 350°F. Toss the portobellos in the olive oil, pepper, and salt and place them on the grill. Grill each side until slightly charred, about 5 minutes per side. Slice the portobellos into 1-inch thick strips. Serve the portobellos with corn tortillas and pickled red onions, or use the portobellos, sauce, and onions as part of another dish, like quesadillas.

Grilled Sweet Potatoes and Fennel
Camotes y Hinojo Asado

MAKES 4 SERVINGS

Sweet potatoes and fennel are perfect companions for the Chile Rub for Grilled Vegetables. A little sweet, a little heat, and a lot of smoky flavor.

2 medium sweet potatoes, sliced into 1/8-inch thick slabs
2 small bulbs fennel, split in half lengthwise
2 tablespoons Garlic-Citrus Olive Oil (page 43) or olive oil
1/4 cup Chile Rub for Grilled Vegetables (page 183)

Light the grill and let the heat reach about 350°F. Brush the sweet potatoes and fennel with the Garlic-Citrus Olive Oil. Rub them with the Chile Rub for Grilled Vegetables. Grill the sweet potatoes on both sides until they develop char lines, about 3 to 4 minutes per side. Grill the fennel cut-side down until it is nearly blackened, about 7 to 8 minutes. Flip and grill another 4 to 5 minutes. Slice into 1-inch strips or serve as is.

Smoked and Grilled Seitan in Pumpkin Seed Tomato Sauce

Seitan al Carbon en Pipián Rojo

MAKES 5 TO 6 SERVINGS

Grilled foods are a guilty pleasure of mine. I'll light my grill to make one thing and end up grilling ingredients for ten different dishes. I just can't resist. It's also the place where I make the heartiest foods, like mushrooms, seitan, tofu, tempeh, and such. Even though I use shredded seitan in this recipe, feel free to use any of the proteins just mentioned or another hearty vegetable of your choice. The sauce is as much the star of this recipe as the seitan.

Pumpkin Seed Tomato Sauce:
4 Roma tomatoes
2 guajillo chiles, rehydrated
1/2 cup toasted salted pepitas
1/4 cup toasted sesame seeds
3 tablespoons white balsamic vinegar
1/8 teaspoon ground cinnamon
3/4 teaspoon salt
2 cloves garlic

Seitan:
3 cups shredded seitan or your favorite meatless strips
1 small white onion, sliced into 1/8-inch thick strips
3 tablespoons olive oil
1/2 teaspoon salt
Juice of 1 orange

Light your grill, preferably using mesquite wood, and let the coals die down until they are low, about 250°F. Grill the tomatoes until the skins are partially blackened and splitting. Remove the tomatoes from the heat and transfer them to a blender along with the guajillos, pepitas, sesame seeds, vinegar, cinnamon, salt, and garlic and purée until smooth. Set aside.

Toss the seitan and onion in the olive oil, salt, and orange juice. Transfer the seitan mixture to a grill pan and place toward the side of the grill. Grill for 1 hour, stirring every 10 minutes. Transfer the seitan and sauce to a large bowl, toss, and serve with corn tortillas or over rice.

Chef's Tip: Make it extra smoky by smoking the seitan in a smoker with mesquite wood for 1 hour. If you do this, you only need to grill it for 20 minutes.

Pit-Roasted Vegetables
Verduras Pibil

MAKES 4 SERVINGS

Pibil-style roasting is traditionally done as a Yucatecan method of cooking where ingredients are placed in a fire pit, covered with maguey leaves, and roasted for hours, often overnight. The food develops a complex texture, crispy in some parts, succulent in others, and completely infused with smoke and whatever flavoring agents are used in the roasting process. I'm assuming you have neither a fire pit nor maguey leaves, so I've developed a method to approximate this cooking technique using a simple cast iron Dutch oven and a regular wood-fire grill. Feel free to mix and match veggies—just make sure they are hearty, so they can withstand the prolonged cook time. It's also a great way to slow-roast meat alternatives or tempeh, if that's your fancy.

Roasting Mix:
2 tablespoons achiote paste
6 cloves garlic, smashed into a paste
Juice of 1 orange
Juice of 1 lime
1/4 cup olive oil
3/4 teaspoon salt

Vegetables:
4 medium zucchini or Mexican gray squash, chopped into 1-inch pieces
1 medium red onion, chopped into 1-inch pieces
2 medium red potatoes, chopped into 1-inch pieces
2 poblano chiles, chopped into 1-inch pieces
1 1/2 cups cooked pinto beans, rinsed

Light the grill and let the coals die down to a medium-low heat, about 300°F. Make a space among the coals that will hold the Dutch oven. You will not need the grill rack.

In a 2-quart Dutch oven, evenly combine the achiote paste, garlic paste, orange juice, lime juice, oil, and salt. Add the zucchini, onion, potatoes, and poblanos and toss. Place the lid on the Dutch oven, but leave it slightly off by about 1/2 inch to allow the smoke to get into the Dutch oven. Place the Dutch oven among the coals. Cook for 2 hours, stirring every 15 to 20 minutes. Serve as is or with corn tortillas and chopped avocado.

Grilled Mexican Spring Onions
Cebollitas Asadas

MAKES 6 TO 8 SERVINGS

Cebollitas are long green onions with medium-size bulbs at the bottom. The entire onion is tossed in oil and grilled, then served whole or sliced as a condiment for tacos and other grilled main dishes. They also make a great topping for enchiladas and many of the antojitos

6 to 8 cebollitas (also known as knob onions)
1 tablespoon olive oil
1/2 teaspoon coarse salt

Toss the cebollitas in the oil and salt and grill until they are soft and lightly browned all around the bulb.

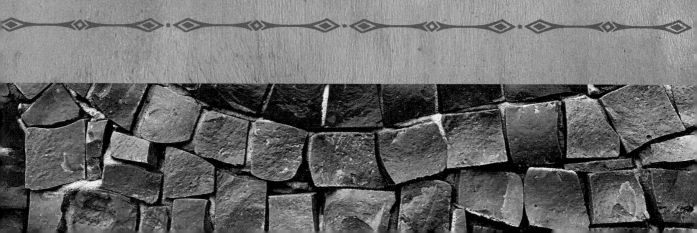

SMALL BITES AND SNACKS

Botanas y Tentempies

Many of these recipes serve multiple purposes as appetizers, snacks, and sides. A few of them take some time to make, but most are fairly quick, and even the ones that take time to make aren't that labor-intensive.

The line between botanas, which are similar to Spanish tapas, and antojitos is blurry at best. In fact, it was sometimes difficult to categorize a recipe as one or the other simply because they are classified as different things depending on where in Mexico you find yourself. Most often, you'll find botanas as small bites at restaurants and bars or as small eats at a wedding celebration rather than on the street. Tentempies, on the other hand, are more like appetizers and quick snacks. Again, it's hard to claim a recipe as one or the other, so I've placed the small-bite recipes all in this one chapter and cleverly declined to categorize them. I'll leave that up to you. Keep in mind that these recipes tend to store well, so you can make them and keep them for several days.

Roasted White Sweet Potatoes with Burnt Chile Sauce
Camotes Blancos Asadas con Chilmole

MAKES 3 1/2 CUPS

I love white sweet potatoes for their lush, sweet flavor. They're absolutely divine on their own, but you can kick them up a bit with this Yucatecan burnt chile sauce. You really don't need anything else.

2 medium white sweet potatoes, peeled if desired and chopped into 1-inch pieces
2 tablespoons olive oil
3/4 teaspoon coarse sea salt
1/2 cup Chilmole (below)

Preheat the oven to 400°F. Toss the sweet potatoes, oil, and salt together in a 9 x 9-inch baking dish. Cover with foil and roast for 30 minutes. Transfer the sweet potatoes to a platter and toss with the Chilmole.

Chilmole

MAKES 1/2 CUP

If you're familiar with this sauce, the name evokes the exotic aroma of burnt seeds and chiles. It violates the basic tenet of stopping short of burning your chiles, yet manages to capture a rustic, sublime, well-balanced flavor. In Yucatán, a local chile is used to make this sauce, but they are hard to come by outside of that state. Instead, you can use a mix of guajillo chiles, ancho chiles, and chiles de árbol to make your sauce.

2 ancho chiles, stemmed and seeded, seeds reserved
2 guajillo chiles, stemmed and seeded, seeds reserved
1 1/2 teaspoons black peppercorns
2 cloves
2 allspice berries

Pinch ground cinnamon

1 teaspoon dried Mexican oregano

4 cloves garlic

1/4 medium white onion, sliced into 1/8-inch thick rings

2 dried chiles de árbol, stemmed

2 corn tortillas

Juice of 1 orange

Juice of 1 lime

3/4 teaspoon salt

In a dry medium pan over medium heat, toast the ancho and guajillo seeds until they are blackened. Set aside. Toast the peppercorns, cloves, allspice, cinnamon, and oregano for 30 seconds. Transfer the ancho seeds, guajillo seeds, peppercorns, cloves, allspice, cinnamon, and Mexican oregano to a spice grinder and grind them (or grind them directly in a blender). Pan-roast the garlic and onion until they are charred, then transfer them to the blender. Either toast or fry the anchos, guajillos, and chiles de árbol and tortillas until blackened. Transfer the anchos, guajillos, and chiles de árbol to a heat-proof bowl and pour hot water over them. Let them rehydrate for 15 minutes. Remove the chiles from the water and transfer them to the blender. Add the orange juice, lime juice, and salt and purée until smooth.

Spiced Green Pumpkin Seeds
Pepitas con Chile de Árbol Molida

MAKES 1 CUP

Think of these like spiced peanuts but made with pepitas and way spicier. You can adjust the heat by using fewer chiles de árbol or using a guajillo chile instead if you want something very mild. Serve with a cold beer and you've got the perfect party combo.

1 cup raw pepitas

1 tablespoon corn oil

1/2 teaspoon salt

6 chiles de árbol, toasted and ground, or 1 teaspoon chile de árbol powder

1/4 teaspoon freshly ground black pepper

2 teaspoons grated piloncillo or turbinado sugar

Heat a medium skillet over medium heat. Add the pepitas, oil, and salt and toast, slowly stirring, until the pepitas are light brown, about 5 minutes. Remove the skillet from the heat and immediately stir the chiles de árbol or chile de árbol powder, pepper, and piloncillo or turbinado sugar into the pepitas. Transfer the pepitas to a bowl and serve.

Plantain Chips with Orange Aioli
Chifles con Crema de Ajo

MAKES 3 CUPS (6 SERVINGS)

Plantain chips, which are basically potato chips made with plantains, are common all throughout Central America. They can be found in convenience stores, in markets, and at many roadside stalls, especially in the south of Mexico. I serve these with a garlic mayo similar to an aioli. (See photo on page 190.)

- **6 cups corn or vegetable oil**
- **2 medium green plantains**
- **Zest of 2 limes**
- **1/2 teaspoon salt**
- **1/2 teaspoon chile de árbol powder or chile powder of your choice**
- **Juice of 2 limes**
- **1/2 cup Crema de Ajo (below)**

In a heavy pot at least 2 inches deep (preferably cast iron), heat the oil to 375°F. While the oil is heating, slice off the ends of the plantains and score the skin lengthwise along both ridges, then peel the plantains. Cut the plantains diagonally into 1/8-inch thick slices. In a large mixing bowl, combine the lime zest, salt, and chile de árbol powder and set aside.

Working in 4 batches, fry the plantains for about 1 minute until they are crisp and golden. Transfer them to a paper towel to drain. Once all the batches have been fried, transfer the plantain chips to the bowl with the zest, salt, and chile de árbol powder. Add the lime juice and toss to combine.

Crema de Ajo
MAKES 1 1/4 CUPS

Crema de ajo is a fusion of Mediterranean garlic dips, like aioli and toum, with the Yucatecan twist of sour orange juice. You can adjust the garlic up or down as you like.

- **6 large cloves garlic**
- **1 cup vegan mayonnaise**
- **1/3 teaspoon salt**
- **1/3 teaspoon freshly ground black pepper**
- **Juice of 1 orange**
- **Juice of 1 lime**

In a blender or food processor, purée the garlic, mayonnaise, salt, pepper, orange juice, and lime juice until smooth.

Stewed Greens
Guisado de Quelites

MAKES 2 1/2 TO 3 CUPS

This simple stew of greens makes a great side, a light lunch, or even a great taco filling. I use quelites, which is a catch-all phrase for different types of wild greens, such as amaranth, when my local Mexican market has them in stock. When it doesn't, I'll use chard or spinach and the dish is just as good. There really aren't any rules when it comes to these types of stews, except that the greens are the prominent feature. This one just happens to be my go-to favorite.

- **1 tablespoon olive oil**
- **1 small white or yellow onion, finely chopped**
- **2 cloves garlic, minced**
- **1 chipotle in adobo, finely chopped**
- **3 Roma tomatoes, coarsely chopped**
- **8 cups coarsely chopped quelites, chard, or other greens**
- **Salt, to taste**

Heat the oil in a large skillet or wok over medium heat. Add the onion and cook until it is translucent. Add the garlic and sauté 2 minutes. Add the chipotle, tomatoes, quelites, and salt and cook until the greens are wilted and the tomatoes are soft. (The amount of time will vary based on the size of your skillet or if you are using a wok.)

Stuffed Chipotles
Chipotles Mecos Rellenos

MAKES 12 STUFFED CHIPOTLES

A simple appetizer, these are firecrackers of heat and flavor. Make sure you have a window open when rehydrating all the chipotles, because your kitchen will get spicy!

- **12 chipotles mecos, rehydrated, stems attached**
- **3/4 cup Pumpkin Seed Tomato Sauce (page 187)**
- **1/4 cup golden raisins**

Gently slice open one side of the rehydrated chipotles, but don't cut all the way to the tip. Pull open the chipotles and use a small knife to remove the seeds as best you can. Fill each chipotle with about 1 tablespoon of Pumpkin Seed Tomato Sauce and 2 to 3 raisins.

Marinated Lima Beans
Ibes en Escabeche

MAKES 2 1/2 TO 3 CUPS

These marinated beans are a bold treat, loaded with heat and an acidic zing, all carried on a backdrop of chayote squash and ibes beans. Ibes are a type of lima bean found in Yucatán, but you needn't be limited to lima beans for this recipe. You can also use butter beans, gigantes, and even chickpeas, though I find butter beans to be the best alternative. This recipe can be served as a snack, a side dish, and even a condiment. What I like about this recipe is that it only takes a few minutes to prepare (though you do need to let the dish sit) and it will last refrigerated for several days. Try it with a simple dish of rice and beans and let the ibes en escabeche shine. You won't be disappointed.

1 chayote, chopped into 1-inch pieces

1 small red onion, sliced paper thin

3 cloves garlic, sliced lengthwise

2 habanero chiles, stemmed, seeded, and sliced into 1/8-inch thick strips

1 1/2 cups cooked lima beans, rinsed

Juice of 3 oranges

Juice of 2 limes

3/4 teaspoon salt

1/2 teaspoon freshly ground black pepper

1/8 teaspoon ground cloves

1/8 teaspoon ground allspice

2 dried bay leaves

1 teaspoon dried Mexican oregano

Boil the chayote in salted water until it is al dente, about 5 minutes, and drain. Transfer the chayote and the onion, garlic, habaneros, beans, orange juice, lime juice, salt, pepper, cloves, allspice, bay leaves, and Mexican oregano to a nonreactive bowl. (If you need to add more orange juice and lime juice, you can do so. Just keep the ratio of 3 oranges to 2 limes intact.) Let the chayote mixture sit for at least 2 hours before serving (ideally, let it marinate for at least 8 hours). Cover and refrigerate if you are going to let it sit longer than 2 hours.

1. Telera
2. Birote salado
3. Pambazo rolls
4. Bolillo
5. Conchas (yellow and pink)
6. Plain concha (cinnamon and sugar)

BREADS

Pan

Bread didn't exist in Mexico before the Spanish brought wheat, but today it is an integral part of Mexican food. How can you have a great torta without bread, or delicious conchas, or wedding cookies? C'est impossible!

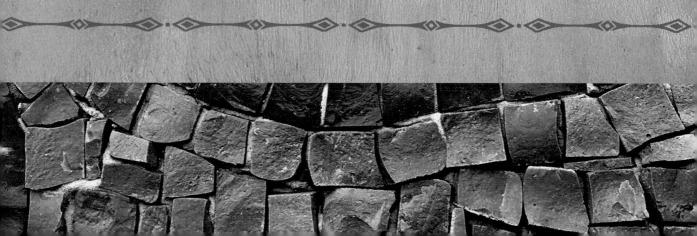

hear you saying, "Get your French out of my Mexican cookbook!" But the history of bread in Mexico is actually the history of its French immigrants. In the late 1700s and early 1800s, Mexico had a strong influx of French nationals, and naturally, they opened patisseries wherever there was a significant (and often not significant) French population.

Originally made to cater to French communities, these breads quickly became popular throughout Mexico, and although many of the French left at the close of the Second Franco-Mexican War in 1867, their bread recipes remained. It's the reason why a Mexican bakery, called a panadería, looks so much like a French bakery (though perhaps a little more colorful).

Nothing remains untouched when cultures meld and collide, treasured recipes included. Many Mexican bread recipes are twists on older French bread recipes, perhaps a little sweeter and a little more colorful. They integrate Central American fruits, such as guavas and mamey, and can be scented with anise and orange, a holdover from when the the Moors conquered Spain. Other recipes use piloncillo for sugar instead of simple table sugar. There are specialty breads for various religious holidays, and Mexicans observe a lot of religious holidays! The tortilla may reign supreme in Mexico, but breads are the close cousins in that royal court.

Sweet Bread
Pan Dulce

MAKES 12 SWEET BREADS

"Pan dulce," literally "sweet bread," is a catch-all term for sweetened bread of various shapes and top designs with a sweetened and often colored glaze on top. They are the quintessential Mexican sweet bread, and, like other Mexican sweet breads, the traditional ones use eggs. But there's no need to use them. Vegan pan dulce is easy to make.

Bread:
2 cups plain unsweetened almond milk
1/4 cup sugar plus 2 tablespoons sugar, divided
1/4 cup brown sugar
1 tablespoon or 1 (.25-ounce) package active dry yeast
1/4 cup vegan shortening
4 cups unbleached all-purpose flour
1/4 cup cornstarch
1 teaspoon salt

Topping:
1/2 cup vegan shortening
1/2 cup confectioners' sugar
1/2 cup granulated sugar

1 tablespoon vanilla extract
Food coloring (see note)

Slowly heat the milk in a medium saucepan over medium-low heat until it becomes warm to the touch (about 110°F to 120°F). Remove the saucepan from the heat. Stir in 1/4 cup of the sugar, brown sugar, and yeast and set aside.

Using an electric mixer, whip together the shortening and the remaining 2 tablespoons of sugar until it creams together. Add the milk mixture. (Mix using the lowest setting on your mixer or you will not have a dough—you will have a mess!)

In a large bowl, combine the flour, cornstarch, and salt. Mix together with a whisk or spoon. Leave a well in the middle. Slowly pour the milk-shortening mixture into the flour well, stirring occasionally. Once the dough is combined, return it to the bowl. Cover it and place it someplace warm to rise for 1 hour.

Divide the dough into 12 portions. Roll each into a ball and flatten it out slightly with your hand until you have something that looks like an uncut hamburger bun. Lightly grease 2 large baking sheets or line them with parchment paper. Place 6 pieces of dough on each sheet, giving them lots of room to expand.

After allowing the bread to rise for 40 minutes, add the topping.

Using an electric mixer, whip together the shortening, confectioners' sugar, granulated sugar, and vanilla for 1 minute. (Start on a low setting or, once again, you will have a mess.) Divide the topping into the number of portions you will need. Dye the topping whatever color you wish.

Divide the topping into 12 parts and roll them into balls. If you have 1 color, make 12 balls; or, if you have 2 colors, make 6 balls of each and so on. Take each of these balls and press it flat between your palms. Carefully place each topping on one of the buns. Using the point of a knife or toothpick, carve an interesting design. Repeat this process until all the buns are topped. Set them to the side and allow the buns to rise 20 more minutes.

Preheat the oven to 350°F. After the 20-minute rise time, transfer the baking sheets to the oven and bake for 15 minutes. Remove the Sweet Bread from the heat and enjoy.

Note: You can add a small amount of beet juice, ground turmeric, or ground annatto seed for some colorful homemade food coloring. You can also purchase all-natural food coloring at health food stores.

Sweet Shell Bread
Conchas

MAKES 12 ROLLS

Conchas are named after the seashell pattern on the top of this sweet bread. They're a type of pan dulce, but conchas are so popular, they deserved their own recipe. Most Mexican bakeries and grocery markets have racks of conchas of different colors waiting to tempt passersby. Unfortunately, most conchas are made with eggs and they go by another name: pan de huevos. In fact, that's what my mom calls them. Enter the vegan concha! These breads are easy to make—you can make them at home and flavor them with different sugars, if you like. Now you no longer need be denied conchas.

Rolls:
1/2 cup water
3/4 cup plain unsweetened almond milk
1 tablespoon or 1 (.25-ounce) package active dry yeast
1/3 cup sugar
3 1/2 to 4 cups unbleached all-purpose flour
1 tablespoon cornstarch
1 teaspoon salt
1/3 cup vegan butter, room temperature

Topping:
1/3 cup sugar
1/4 cup vegan butter or vegan shortening
1/2 cup unbleached all-purpose flour
1 teaspoon ground cinnamon
1/2 teaspoon vanilla extract
1 1/2 teaspoons orange zest
2 to 3 drops food coloring, optional

Heat the water and milk in a small saucepanover medium heat until it feels warm to the touch, about 110°F to 120°F. Remove the saucepan from the heat and add the yeast and sugar. Stir this together and set aside.

In a large bowl, whisk together 3 1/2 cups of the flour with the cornstarch, and salt. Add the butter and use a fork or your hands to crumble it into the flour. Once the butter is crumbled in, add the milk mixture slowly and knead the dough until it is smooth. If the dough is sticky to the touch, add extra flour, 1/4 cup at a time, until it is no longer sticky.

Lightly flour a clean work surface and knead the dough 5 minutes. Transfer the dough to a lightly oiled bowl and allow the dough to rise in a warm place for 1 1/2 hours. While it is rising, make the topping.

Using a bowl and mixer, beat the sugar and butter or shortening until they are completely creamed together. Add the flour and stir until it forms a dough. Separate the dough into 3 small bowls. To the first bowl add the cinnamon, to the second bowl add the vanilla, and to third bowl add the orange zest. Mix the different doughs to work their respective flavorings throughout then shape each of the dough portions into

4 balls and set aside. If you want a colored concha, add 2 to 3 drops food coloring to the dough. Cover the bowls with plastic wrap and let sit.

After 1 1/2 hours, punch down the dough. Divide the dough into 12 pieces and shape it into balls. Line 2 baking sheets with parchment paper and place the dough balls on those sheets. Take 1 round of topping and pat it into a 3-inch round. Use it to cover one of the dough balls. Repeat this process until all the conchas are covered. Make 5 to 6 cuts across the dough using a table knife in a rough shell pattern. Allow the dough to rise somewhere warm for 40 minutes.

Preheat the oven to 375°F. Bake the buns for 20 minutes, until they are golden brown. Allow them to cool before serving.

Cinnamon Fritters
Buñuelos

MAKES 20 FRITTERS

These fritters are like large flat doughnuts laced with anise and dressed with cinnamon and sugar (although in the south of Mexico, they look more like doughnut holes than flat discs). Buñuelos were originally a treat enjoyed by Spanish Moors. Like so many things Spanish that were introduced to Mexico, they became a fusion of local cuisine, as evidenced by the optional piloncillo and Guava Syrup. Buñuelos are usually served at fairs and around major religious holidays.

3 cups unbleached all-purpose flour, plus 1/4 cup flour for rolling the dough

2 tablespoons cornstarch

1 tablespoon baking powder

1 tablespoon salt

1 tablespoon sugar

1/4 teaspoon ground anise

1 1/4 cups plain unsweetened almond or soy milk

1/2 cup vegan butter or vegan shortening

Corn oil, for frying

1/4 cup sugar combined with 1 teaspoon ground cinnamon

Optional Guava Syrup:
6 ounces piloncillo

3 1/2 cups water, divided

1 (4-inch) cinnamon stick

6 ripe medium guavas, puréed

1/4 teaspoon ground anise

Zest of 1 orange

In a large bowl, combine the flour, cornstarch, baking powder, salt, sugar, and anise. Create a well in the middle of the flour mixture and set aside. Add the milk and butter. Knead the dough until it is very smooth. This will take a bit of time. Once the dough is smooth, shape it into 20 balls. Place the balls on a baking sheet lined with parchment paper. Drape plastic wrap over them and allow them to rest for 30 minutes.

After 30 minutes, add at least 1 inch of oil to a large, deep skillet and heat it to 360°F. Lightly flour a clean work surface and roll each ball into a 6-inch disc. Place each ball in the oil and fry each side until it is light golden brown. Remove it from the oil and place it on an absorbent towel. Sprinkle the ball with the cinnamon sugar. Repeat this process until all the dough is fried.

To make the optional Guava Syrup, melt the piloncillo with 1 cup of the water over medium-high heat in a small pot and cook until it turns into thin caramel. Stir in the remaining 2 1/2 cups water, cinnamon stick, and the puréed guavas, anise, and orange zest and cook for 6 minutes. Remove the Guava Syrup from the heat and allow it to cool until warm. Smother the Cinnamon Fritters in the syrup.

Bolillos and Birote Salado

MAKES 10 ROLLS

Bolillos are basically crusty oval sour French sandwich baguettes. Bolillos are also known as *pan francés*—French bread. When they come out of the oven, knock on them and listen for the hollow sound that indicates that you've got a good bolillo. Birote salado is a close variation of the bolillo from Guadalajara and is the classic bread used for tortas ahogadas. It's named after the Birrott family, a French family that owned a bakery in Guadalajara in the mid-1800s. It's a little saltier than a typical bolillo and a little heartier as well. It's said that the altitude and climate of Guadalajara help make the bread, but I can attest you can still make a great birote salado outside of that city. The only difference in the two recipes is the level of salt used, a slight adjustment to the baking time and temperature, and the amount of time the sourdough starter ferments.

> 1 tablespoon or 1 (.25-ounce) package active dry yeast, divided
> 2 cups warm water, divided
> 4 cups unbleached all-purpose flour or 2 cups unbleached all-purpose
>   flour mixed with 2 cups whole-wheat flour, divided
> 1 teaspoon sugar
> 1 teaspoon salt for bolillos or 1 3/4 teaspoon salt for birote salado
> 1/4 cup plain unsweetened almond or soy milk

In a medium mixing bowl, combine 1/2 teaspoon of the yeast with 1/2 cup of the warm water and 3/4 cup of the flour. Cover the bowl with plastic wrap and let it sit unrefrigerated for 8 to 24 hours. For birote salado, the rest time is only 6 hours. This is your sourdough starter.

Once the sourdough starter is ready, it's time to make the dough and bake it. Heat the remaining 1 1/2 cups water in a small pot over medium-low heat until it is warm to the touch, about 110°F to 120°F. Remove the water from the heat and add the sugar and the remaining 2 1/2 teaspoons yeast. Stir to combine and allow the water mixture to sit at least 5 minutes.

In a large bowl, combine the remaining 3 1/4 cups flour with the salt. Stir the flour gently and form a well in the middle. Add the warm water mixture. Knead the dough on a clean, lightly floured work surface for 10 minutes until it is smooth. Transfer the dough back to the bowl, cover the bowl, and place it in a warm place to rise for 1 hour.

After 1 hour, punch the dough down. Knead it for 1 minute, then cut the dough into 10 portions. Shape each piece into a cylindrical shape, with the ends slightly tapered. To shape the dough, cup your hands over the cylinder of dough and rock your hands back and forth. Line 2 baking sheets with parchment paper and place the rolls on them. Allow the rolls to rise for about 30 minutes.

Preheat the oven to 450°F for bolillos and 480°F for birote salado. Place a metal oven-proof bowl with 1 1/2 cups of water in it on the floor of the oven. Make a shallow slit down the center of each roll, holding the knife at a 45-degree angle. Brush each roll with some of the milk. The steam created by the water in the bowl gives the bolillos their crust. Bake the rolls for 25 minutes for bolillos and 15 minutes for birote salado. Remove the bread from the oven and allow the rolls to cool before using them.

Telera Rolls
Pan Telera

MAKES 10 ROLLS

Telera rolls are classic sandwich breads for tortas, a little chewy on the outside and soft on the inside. Their classic shape is mostly round, slightly tapered at the ends, with three humps on top.

- **1 1/2 cups plain unsweetened almond milk or soy milk or water**
- **2 teaspoons or 1 (.25-ounce) package active dry yeast**
- **1 tablespoon sugar**
- **1 tablespoon vegan butter or vegan shortening, melted and cooled**
- **1 1/2 teaspoons salt**
- **3 1/2 to 4 cups unbleached all-purpose flour or 1 1/2 cups unbleached all-purpose flour combined with 2 cups whole-wheat flour**
- **2 to 3 tablespoons plain unsweetened almond or soy milk mixed with 1 teaspoon cornstarch**

Warm the milk or water in a small saucepan over medium heat until it is warm to the touch but not hot, about 110°F to 120°F. Remove the saucepan from the heat and add the yeast and sugar. Stir to combine and set aside. Melt the butter or shortening in a small pot over medium-low heat, then remove from the heat to cool.

Add the salt and 3 1/2 cups of the flour in a large bowl. Stir the salt and flour together, but leave a well in the center. Add the cooled butter or shortening to the milk mixture and pour this into the well. Mix the dry and wet ingredients using a heavy spoon, then knead the dough until it is completely smooth and notsticky to the touch. If it is sticky, add the remaining flour, 1/4 cup at a time, and continue mixing until the dough is smooth. On a clean work surface, sprinkle 1 tablespoon flour and transfer the dough to the work surface. Knead the dough 10 minutes. Place it back in the bowl, cover the bowl, and place it in a warm place to rise for 1 hour.

After 1 hour, the dough should be doubled in size. Knead the dough a few times, then cut it into 10 pieces. Preheat the oven to 400°F. Line 2 baking sheets with parchment paper. Shape each of the 10 pieces into a football shape that tapers at the ends. Place the rolls on the prepared baking sheets and allow them to double in size.

Once the rolls have doubled in size once more, score them twice on the tops so that you create 3 sections of equal proportion. Brush the tops with the milk-cornstarch mixture. Place the rolls in the oven and bake them for 20 minutes, until the outside is light golden brown. Remove the buns from the oven and allow them to cool before using.

Little Piggies Shortbread Cookies
Puercitos

MAKES 40 COOKIES

These cookies are found all over Mexico under a wide variety of names like cochinitos and cerditos, but they're pretty much all the same and they're always shaped like little pigs; hence, the name. They're more bready than crispy, like a shortbread, but the sweetener used in them is piloncillo, which gives them a distinctive taste. And they are oh, so soft and fluffy. If you don't eat them all right away—a difficult task to resist—jar them so they don't dry out and put them well out of sight, lest temptation get the better of you. You'll need a pig-shaped cookie cutter, which you can find online and at most Mexican markets, but if you don't have one, you can make them whatever shape you like.

10 to 12 ounces piloncillo, preferably chopped or in small cones, or 1 1/2 to 2 cups brown sugar, to taste

1 (4-inch) cinnamon stick or 1 teaspoon ground cinnamon

3 tablespoons agave syrup

3/4 cup water

2 sticks (1 cup) vegan butter

4 1/2 cups unbleached all-purpose flour or whole-wheat pastry flour

1 teaspoon baking powder

1 teaspoon baking soda

2/3 teaspoon salt

1/4 cup applesauce

1 tablespoon water mixed with 1 1/2 teaspoons cornstarch

Confectioners' sugar

Simmer the piloncillo or brown sugar, cinnamon stick, agave, and water in a small saucepan over medium-low heat for 15 to 20 minutes, until the mixture reaches the consistency of light syrup. Remove the cinnamon stick and add the butter, stirring until it melts.

In a large mixing bowl, combine the flour, baking powder, baking soda, and salt and make a well in the center. Pour the sugar mixture and applesauce into the well and incorporate the wet and dry ingredients. The dough should be sticky. Cover the bowl with plastic wrap and refrigerate for 4 to 8 hours.

Preheat the oven to 375°F and lightly grease a baking sheet or line it with a silicone mat. Transfer the dough to a lightly floured work surface and roll the dough out about 1/4 inch thick. Use a pig-shaped cookie cutter that is about 3 to 4 inches in length to cut out the cookies. Transfer the cookies to the baking sheet and brush them with the water-cornstarch mixture. Bake the cookies for 8 to 9 minutes and sprinkle them with the confectioners' sugar when you remove them from the oven.

DRINKS

Bebidas

A good drink should make you smile, and Mexico is full of great drinks. I'm not just talking about alcoholic drinks, either, so put down the tequila for now.

With so much flavorful fresh fruit, it's easy to simply whirl it up in a blender with a little water and get the perfect drink for a hot afternoon or a spicy meal. Then there are the coffees, the drinks made from blended nuts or grains, the sodas made with pure cane sugar, the spicy drinks, the chile-flavored hot chocolate, and many more. Volumes could be written on the enormous variety of drinks, but a couple of themes emerge. First, they pop with flavor, just like most other Mexican food. They feel lively. Second, they tend to perk you up, whether through sweetness, spiciness, caffeine, or some other component. Most drinks, even the alcohol-based ones, have components to refresh and pick you up.

Aguas Frescas

I firmly believe agua frescas are a one of the true treasures of Mexico. Not many people outside of Latin America have heard of them, but they are certainly growing in popularity. In Mexico, I don't think they can get any more popular, and for good reason. These drinks are usually made with fresh fruit or melons. Sometimes sugar is added to the drink, but if the main ingredient is sweet enough, then the only other ingredient in the agua fresca is water. Just imagine pouring liquid mango, the sweetest one you've tasted, over ice and having that as your afternoon refreshment. That's an agua fresca. Be aware that some agua frescas you can buy at the market or street stalls are sweetened with honey, and there's no general rule determining which one is and which one isn't. Of course, like all Mexican food categories, there are those tasty miscreants that defy the category, like the cucumber chile agua fresca. They're all good, and that's what matters.

Refreshing Drinks

Mexico also boasts shaved-ice treats called raspados, more similar to the Italian granita than a snow cone. The best ones are made with fresh juices and fruit purées, while the lower-end ones are made with food coloring, artificial flavors, and sugar. These are popular street-food snacks that you can easily make at home. You don't need a shaved-ice maker, just a fork, a bowl, and the right technique. There are also refrescas, which are usually carbonated beverages like chilled sodas, but they are not always carbonated. They could be lemonade, a chilled beet-flavored beverage, or something like the coconut and corn drink found in this book.

Festival Drinks

Then there are the drinks thickened with masa, called atoles, the most famous of which is champurrado, Mexico's national hot chocolate. Atoles can be thin or thick like pudding, and it's totally dependent on individual tastes. I've made chocolate atole for a class with several Mexican students and one student complained that the atole was too thick and another complained the atole wasn't thick enough! Make it how you like it. Chocolate isn't the only atole—there are also atoles made from pineapple, blackberries, strawberries, chiles, and simply vanilla and piloncillo. A cousin to the atole is pozol, which is an atole in every manner save that the masa is lightly fermented. Lucky for you, you've now got recipes for all of those!

Mexican Tequila and Mezcal

Tequila is a distilled drink made by steaming and crushing agave hearts (called pinas), extracting the syrup, and distilling it. Tequila blanco has the cleanest, simplest taste and is only fermented for a few weeks. Tequila reposado is aged for a couple months and develops a deeper, more complex flavor. Both of these are good tequilas to use in mixed drinks. Tequila anejo is aged tequila, which can be aged for a couple of years and has brandy-like qualities. Tequila anejo is best used as sipping tequila. Mezcal—which is the granddaddy of tequila and is currently seeing a surge in interest in the United States—is made in a similar way to tequila, but the agave hearts are first fire-roasted, giving the drink a smoky flavor. It's usually aged longer than tequila. Mezcal is almost always a sipping drink. Most mezcals are produced on small farms as opposed to mass-produced tequilas. My advice for tequilas and mezcals is to spend the money on the sipping drinks and go for a midgrade quality for mixed drinks. (For more details about tequila, mezcal, and beer, check out the drink section in my book, *Vegan Tacos: Authentic and Inspired Recipes for Mexico's Favorite Street Food.*)

Mexican Wines

Mexico is becoming known for is its burgeoning wine industry. Several regions are perfect for growing grapes, and these regions produce some of the best wines in the world. However, because these wines don't have long-established reputations behind them right now, they tend to be less expensive than their European and Californian counterparts. Wine is a relatively new product for Mexico; however, the first large vineyard was planted in 1791 at the Santo Tomás de Aquino Mission in Baja (of course, it was a mission). Certainly, wines were being made soon after the Spanish brought over grapes in the sixteenth century. Legend says that Hernan Cortes, as one of his first acts as governor of Mexico, ordered grapevines to be brought over from Spain and planted all over Mexico. Wines were produced on a small scale, but production started to ramp up by the early 1800s. Unfortunately, the Mexican civil war devastated Mexico's wine production. It never recovered enough to reach great heights until sommelier Hugo d'Acosta made a concerted effort to up the game in Mexican wine making in the Guadalupe Valley of Baja. Now Baja is well known for its high-quality wines and produces about 90 percent of all the wines in Mexico.

There are other regions in Mexico that produce good-quality wines, even if their production level isn't nearly the same as Baja. The other one of particular note is Aguascaliente, which produces some fantastic sparkling reds and whites and several spiced wines, which make appearances in many of that region's dishes. If you can find any of these wines, I strongly suggest trying them. If you're looking for a unique vacation, I recommend visiting either of these wine-producing regions in Mexico and making a food and wine tour out of it. You will not be disappointed. Salud!

Make Your Own Agua Fresca

Making a spur-of-the-moment agua fresca is easy. Simply combine 4 cups of coarsely chopped fruit, melon, or berries, 4 cups water, and sweetener to taste in a blender. Blend until smooth and serve over ice. Some of my favorites include mango, apple, tamarind, banana, guava, watermelon, and cantaloupe. Following are some other agua frescas you can try.

Spinach and Pineapple Agua Fresca
Agua Fresca de Piña y Espinicas

MAKES 7 TO 8 CUPS

I am not a fan of greens in drinks and smoothies, so I was reluctant to try this when I first saw it show up at my local Mexican market. Spinach in a drink? Not so sure about that, but I'm willing to try anything vegan once. I'll just say I am now a total convert. This agua fresca is one of the best ones I've had. Sweet, refreshing, and just the right blend of sweetness and herbaciousness. You'll want to vary the amount of agave used in the recipe based on how sweet your pineapple is. Serve this in a big cup over ice and make enough for seconds!

    4 cups coarsely chopped pineapple
    4 cups baby spinach leaves
    4 cups water
    Agave syrup, to taste

Combine the pineapple, spinach, water, and agave in a blender. Purée until smooth and serve over ice.

Cucumber Agua Fresca
Agua Fresca de Pepino

MAKES 6 CUPS

This is not your typical agua fresca. While nearly all of them are sweet and made from some sort of fruit or melon, this is a spicy, salty drink. It took me aback the first time I tried it, because I was expecting sweetness. But I quickly grew to crave the interplay of freshness and spiciness. Like all agua frescas, this should be served over ice.

2 chiles de árbol
1/2 teaspoon salt
2 large cucumbers, peeled and coarsely chopped
1 tablespoon chopped fresh mint
Juice of 3 limes
4 cups water, divided

In a blender, grind the chiles de árbol and salt until they reach a coarse texture. Add the cucumbers, mint, lime juice, and 2 cups of the water. Blend until smooth. Add the remaining 2 cups water and blend one more time. Serve over ice.

Salted Beer and Tomato Lime Juice
Michelada

MAKES 1 MICHELADA

The first time I saw this concoction of beer and tomato juice, I thought, "What is that monstrosity?" One night a friend brought over V8 Vegetable Juice and Schlitz Malt Liquor. I refused to touch the stuff. When I saw the real deal in Mexico, I finally broke down and tried it. What an experience! Intense, made with fresh ingredients, loaded with hot sauce. It was incredible. I am now a michelada fan, but be warned that the drink is intense and relies heavily on good-quality ingredients. There are plenty of variations of this drink all around Mexico, but this is the most popular version served in Mexico City (and is said to cure hangovers). I'm not sure about that last part, but the chile and lime go a long way to perking one up!

Juice of 2 limes
1/3 teaspoon coarse sea salt plus more for the rim of the glass
2 Roma tomatoes, coarsely chopped
2 tablespoons pequín chile hot sauce or hot sauce of your choice
1 (8-ounce) bottle lager or light, crisp beer

Dip the rim a glass in the lime juice and press the wet rim into a dish of coarse sea salt. In a food processor, purée the lime juice, salt, tomatoes, and hot sauce. Combine the tomato mixture with the beer and pour into a glass, making sure not to disturb the salted glass rim.

Coconut Corn Drink
Pozol de Coco

MAKES 4 1/2 CUPS

Pozol is a hot drink made with fermented masa, and there are quite a few variations on this. In a way, it's like a fermented atole. Most pozol drinks are sweet, though some eschew the sugar and go for spicy! One of my favorite unsweetened ones is pozol blanco from Chiapas, which utilizes chiles, salt, and lemons. The one below is my favorite sweet one, made with sugar and coconut milk. It's very easy to make, but it does take a week for the corn dough to ferment. The drink is ideal to make if you have masa left over from making tortillas that's been in your refrigerator for a few days, because that's how long it takes for the masa to safely ferment. If you don't have fermented masa, simply add a shot of tequila. No one will blame you.

1/2 cup fermented masa (see note)

3 cups canned coconut milk

1 cup water

1/2 cup piloncillo or turbinado sugar

Zest of 2 limes

2 tablespoons tequila, optional

Combine the masa, milk, water, piloncillo or turbinado sugar, lime zest, and tequila (if using) to a small pot and simmer for 5 minutes, stirring to make sure the masa evenly combines with the coconut milk. Serve hot or at room temperature.

Note: Fermented masa will have a slight sour smell to it.

Masa-Thickened Spiced Drinks
Atoles

MAKES 3 1/2 CUPS

Corn and masa play such an important role in Mexican cuisine, even drinks make use of it. These drinks, called atoles, are thickened with the same masa used to make tortillas, and they range in thickness from just slightly thick to a pudding-like consistency, based on taste. I like mine more on the thin side, but you can make yours however you like. The most famous atole is champurrado, a type of Mexican hot chocolate, but there are plenty of other versions using just spices and some with puréed fruits or berries. Below is the basic atole with modifications that follow for other popular atoles.

- **1/2 cup masa harina**
- **3 cups plain unsweetened almond milk**
- **1 (3-ounce) piece piloncillo or 1/4 cup brown sugar**
- **1/4 teaspoon salt**

Bring a small pan to medium heat and add the masa harina. Toast the masa harina for 1 minute. Slowly stir in the milk, making sure the masa and milk are evenly combined. Add the piloncillo or brown sugar and salt and simmer for 5 minutes. Transfer the atole to cups and froth using a whisk or molinillo (a wooden frother with rough bulb at the end specifically for frothing atoles).

Variations

Vanilla Cinnamon Atole

- **1 vanilla bean, split lengthwise**
- **1 (3-inch) cinnamon stick**
- **1/2 cup plain unsweetened almond milk**

Add the vanilla bean, cinnamon stick, and milk to the milk in the basic atole recipe and simmer for 10 minutes instead of 5 minutes. Remove and discard the vanilla bean and cinnamon stick before serving.

Orange Zest Atole

- **Zest of 1 orange**
- **2 star anise**
- **1/2 cup plain unsweetened almond milk**

Add the orange zest, star anise, and milk to the milk in the basic atole recipe and simmer for 10 minutes instead of 5 minutes. Remove and discard the star anise before serving.

Peanut Atole

1/2 cup creamy peanut butter
1/2 cup plain unsweetened almond milk
1 small ancho chile

Add the peanut butter, milk, and ancho to the milk in the basic atole recipe and simmer for 10 minutes instead of 5 minutes. Remove and discard the ancho before serving.

Fruit and Berry Atole

1 cup puréed strawberries, blackberries, or pineapple

Press the puréed strawberries, blackberries, or pineapple through a fine-mesh sieve for a smooth texture. Add to the milk in the basic atole recipe.

Muddled Sage Margarita
Margarita de Salvia

MAKES 4 MARGARITAS

It's not a Mexican cookbook without a margarita, but margarita recipes are easy to come by. This is a twist on the classic, with a dry, herbaceous undertone that makes the drink both refreshing and interesting. It forgoes the typical orange liqueur in order to heighten the dry sensation. You'll want a midgrade tequila for this recipe, and if you want to get serious, use mezcal instead of tequila.

1 cup fresh lime juice
Salt, for glass rims
6 leaves fresh sage (preferably golden sage)
4 shots tequila blanco or reposado
3 tablespoons agave nectar

Dip the rims of 4 glasses in the lime juice, then press the wet rims into a plate of salt. Set the glasses aside. Muddle the sage and transfer it to a shaker. Add the lime juice, tequila or reposado, and agave and shake until thoroughly combined. Add a few cubes of ice to each glass and pour the margaritas into the glasses.

Aztec Chocolate
Xocolatl

MAKES 3 1/2 CUPS

This is not your regular hot chocolate drink. It's bitter and spicy, and it's the origin of modern hot chocolate. The word "xocolatl" is a Nahuatl word meaning "bitter water." The Mayans were the first culture to make this drink of sacred beans (Quetzacoatl, the feathered serpent god, was said to have given cacao beans to humans). They mixed it with chiles and cornmeal and used the pulp of fermented cacao beans, which made the drink both sweet and slightly alcoholic, and served it hot. As the Aztecs took over, they demanded tribute in the form of cacao beans, which they couldn't grow themselves. The drink they made from these beans was similar to the Mayan version, but they used the whole bean instead of just the pulp, which made the drink bitter, and they drank their xocalatl cold. I suspect it's because they didn't know how the Mayans made the drink and were making it according to their best guess, as so often happens when food migrates between cultures.

- 1/2 cup masa harina
- 3 cups water
- 2 chiles de árbol or 1 ancho chile (for a milder flavor)
- 2 ounces bitter dark chocolate

Heat the masa harina in a small pan over medium heat for 1 minute. Slowly stir in the water until the mix is smooth. Add the chiles de árbol or ancho and simmer for 5 minutes. Remove the chiles de árbol or ancho and add the chocolate, stirring to melt it. Remove the pan from the heat and allow the drink to come to room temperature.

Roasted Cacao Beans

Aztec Chocolate was originally made with roasted cacao beans and while it's more labor-intensive to do so, it's also very rewarding. Instead of using chocolate, roast 1/4 cup cacao beans in a comal or pan over medium heat, until about half of them pop. Grind them using a mortar and pestle until you have a rough paste. Allow them to sit for 24 hours. Make the drink according to the Aztec Chocolate recipe, substituting this paste for the chocolate. It is an intense, flavorful experience!

Mexican Hot Chocolate with Tequila Anejo
Champurrado con Tequila Anejo

MAKES 2 SERVINGS

Champurrado is the sweet descendant of xocolatl, the spicy, bitter chocolate drink of the Aztecs. Unlike xocolatl, which is served cold, bitter, and spicy, champurrado is a dark, foamy, sweet, chocolate ambrosia. If you think that sounds like more fun, I am inclined to agree with you. During festivals, particularly Día de Los Muertos, the streets are crowded with vendors selling champurrado in Styrofoam cups or plastic bags pierced with a straw. It's the ultimate Mexican street drink. I add a shot of tequila anejo for a more adult version, and, as an admitted chile addict, I add a little ancho powder and chile de árbol powder on top.

- 2 1/4 cups plain unsweetened almond milk
- 1 (2-inch) cinnamon stick
- 1 vanilla bean, split lengthwise, or 1 teaspoon vanilla extract
- 4 ounces Mexican chocolate or a good-quality bittersweet chocolate
- 1/4 cup masa harina
- 2 ounces piloncillo or 3 tablespoons brown sugar
- 2 tablespoons tequila anejo
- 1 teaspoon ancho powder plus pinch chile de árbol powder, optional

Bring the milk to a simmer in a medium pot over medium heat. Add the cinnamon stick and vanilla bean or extract and simmer for 5 minutes. Remove and discard the cinnamon stick and vanilla bean (if using). Add the Mexican chocolate or bittersweet chocolate, masa harina, and piloncillo or brown sugar and slowly stir until the chocolate is melted and the masa harina is no longer lumpy. Remove the hot chocolate from the heat and add the tequila. Quickly rub a molinillo or whisk back and forth between your hands, making it spin in the pot until the hot chocolate foams. Serve immediately and sprinkle the ancho and chile de árbol powder on top (if using).

Candied Pumpkin (page 222)

SWEETS

Dulces

◇

In this chapter, I provide several iconic dessert recipes that are easy to do at home, with instructions on how to make your own variations on them.

exican sweets can be highly complex or as simple as frozen puréed fruit. They sometimes use ingredients you wouldn't expect, like chiles, herbs, and corn (because corn is everywhere), and they run the gamut from French-style pastries to dessert tamales to fresh-fruit popsicles. The treats are always lively, usually sweet, and they make good use of all the high-quality produce available in Mexico. While Mexican desserts certainly have their share of fried foods and heavy cream-laden cakes, there seems to be a larger selection of light, refreshing desserts than show up in many other cuisines. Some of these are eaten at the end of a meal, but many of them are meant to be refreshing snacks throughout the day. That's the kind of sweet treat I like. If you want to create your own paletas or your own churros, you've now got the tools to do so. Have fun with them!

Candied Pumpkin
Calabaza en Tacha

MAKES 6 CUPS

Candied pumpkin, sweet potatoes, coconut, and other similar items are popular all across Mexico. Walk down the market streets of Nogales or Mexico City, and you'll find someone selling these candied treats, particularly the candied pumpkin. These store easily, and you'll probably end up making more than you can eat in one serving. Just seal them in a plastic bag, pressing out as much air as possible, and you can store them in your pantry for several months.

4 cups water
1 (4-inch) cinnamon stick or 1 teaspoon ground cinnamon
8 ounces piloncillo or 2 cups brown sugar
1/4 teaspoon salt
6 cups (1-inch) peeled pumpkin pieces

In a medium pot, bring the water to a simmer over medium heat, add the cinnamon stick or ground cinnamon, piloncillo or brown sugar, and salt, stirring until the sugar has melted. Add the pumpkin and simmer until the pumpkin is soft and the syrup has caramelized around the pumpkin. Remove the candied pumpkin from the pot, place it on wax paper, and allow it to cool. I suggest immediately washing the pot so the sugar doesn't stick to it.

Coconut Rice Pudding
Arroz con Leche de Coco

MAKES 5 SERVINGS

Rice pudding is one of those recipes that's easy to make and even easier to eat! At its heart, it's simply rice, milk (my version uses coconut milk), and sugar. There are, however, a few ingredients and tricks you can use to take it from wholesome goodness to swoon-worthy ecstasy. First is making sure you have a short-grain rice like Arborio or sushi rice, so the dessert gets a little sticky. Second is making sure to use high-quality ingredients. Splurge a little on this one. It's worth it! Your rice pudding should taste aromatic and sweet but not overly sweet, and it should be a little soupy.

3 cups canned unsweetened coconut milk
1/2 cup grated piloncillo or turbinado sugar
1/4 teaspoon salt
1 (4-inch) cinnamon stick (preferably Mexican canela)
1 vanilla bean, split lengthwise
1 tablespoon lemon zest
1 cup short-grain white or brown rice
2 cascabel chiles, optional

In a small pot, bring the coconut milk to a simmer over medium heat and melt the piloncillo or turbinado sugar into it. Add the salt, cinnamon stick, vanilla bean, lemon zest, rice, and cascabels (if using), bring to a simmer, cover the pot, lower the heat to low, and cook for 20 minutes (add 5 minutes to the cooking time if you are using brown rice).

Mexican Ice Pops
Paletas

MAKES 6 TO 8 PALETAS

Gourmet popsicle shops have become a new trend in the United States, but Mexico had the jump on that movement a few decades ago. The plethora of pops available throughout Mexico is staggering, and they're typically made with fresh ingredients. It's no coincidence that a country known for searing summer days and an abundance of high-quality fresh fruit and produce has the popsicle, called a paleta, nailed down. If it's a fruit or a plant, chances are it's been turned into a paleta at some point. Even better, you can make these at home with simply a blender, freezer, and popsicle mold. I prefer using silicone molds, because they make extracting the paletas incredibly easy. Try any of the following combinations.

Blackberry-Coconut Paletas
1 cup sugar, melted into 1 cup coconut milk
2 tablespoons lime juice
1 cup blackberry purée
1 cup mashed blackberries

Pineapple Paletas
1/2 cup sugar, melted into 1 cup water
1 cup puréed pineapple

Mango, Lime, and Chile Paletas
1/2 cup sugar, melted into 1 cup water
Juice of 2 limes
1 cup puréed mango
1/4 teaspoon chile de árbol powder

Creamy Lemon and Corn Paletas
1/2 cup sugar, melted into 1 cup coconut milk
1/2 cup puréed cashews
1/2 cup puréed sweet corn
1/2 cup fresh lemon juice

Horchata Paletas
1/2 cup sugar, melted into 1 cup rice milk
1/4 cup vegan creamer
1/2 teaspoon vanilla extract
1/2 teaspoon ground cinnamon

Hibiscus Paletas
    1 cup hibiscus flowers brewed in 4 cups water, flowers removed
    1 cup sugar
    Juice of 1 orange
    Juice of 1 lime

To Prepare the Paletas

Once you have the desired paleta mix made, pour it into the popsicle molds and transfer them to the freezer. In all cases, whether you are using the recipes in this book or creating your own paletas, you'll need popsicle sticks, and you insert these only when the paletas are partially frozen so that the stick does not tilt to the side. To remove the paleta from the mold, take it out of the freezer and let it sit for about 5 minutes before unmolding it.

Create Your Own Paletas

You can create your own paleta flavor by mixing 1 cup strained fruit or berry purée or juice with 1/2 cup sugar melted into 1 cup water (or coconut milk, for a creamy version). For additional texture, smash a bit of the fruit or berries and add that to the finished mix.

Limes Stuffed with Coconut
Limones Rellenos de Coco

MAKES 6 STANDARD LIMES OR 15 KEY LIMES

This traditional Mexican dessert or snack is a simple, refreshing treat. The secret is to get as much bitterness out of the peel of the limes as possible. Key limes are the most common lime used to make these, but because they are so small, they require significantly more work than if you used standard limes.

6 limes or 15 Key limes
4 cups water, plus more as needed
1/2 cup sugar
1/2 cup sweetened grated coconut

Place the limes in a medium pot with enough water to cover and bring to a boil over medium heat. Boil for 10 minutes, then drain. Repeat this process 2 more times, draining and then replacing the water each time. Doing this in stages is important, because you are leeching the bitterness from the limes with each boil, and then discarding the bitter water. Add the 4 cups of water to the pot, bring it to a boil, and dissolve the sugar into it. Add the limes and boil 10 minutes, then discard the water.

Make a slice halfway into each lime and gently scrape out the fleshy part, leaving the peel intact. Stuff each lime with as much sweetened coconut as will fit and serve.

Peanut Sorbet
Sorbete de Cacahuate

MAKES 4 CUPS

My love for peanut butter knows no bounds, so a recipe for peanut butter sorbet? I'm in! This recipe is incredibly simple to make, and I love the hint of spiciness and orange zest that goes with it. Dip scoops of it in melted chocolate when you're done, refreeze it, and you've basically got a spicy peanut butter cup for dessert.

2 cups turbinado sugar
2 cups water, plus more as needed
Zest of 1 orange
1 chile de árbol
1 1/2 cups chunky salted peanut butter

In a small pot over medium-low heat, dissolve the sugar in the water. Once the sugar is dissolved, add the orange zest and chile de árbol and bring the mixture to a boil. Boil until the sugar caramelizes, then add enough water to the pot to bring the level back to 2 cups. Remove the chile de árbol. Stir in the peanut butter until evenly combined. Either process the mixture in an ice cream maker according to the ice cream maker's instructions or freeze it in a freezer-safe bowl, stirring it every 20 minutes to ensure it doesn't form ice crystals.

Corn Ice Cream with Candied Pecans
Helado de Elote con Pacanas en Tacha

MAKES 3 CUPS

Corn ice cream has been available in Mexico since the early 1900s, but it was a fourteen-year-old Italian immigrant who merged Italian gelato-making with sweetened corn. His shop, Chiandoni, changed the way corn ice cream was made, creating a rich, thick gelato with a delicate flavor that suffuses the entire dessert. To this day, corn ice cream is hugely popular in Mexico City. I make my own version using cashew cream to create the rich backdrop for the ice cream, and I top mine with salted bourbon pecans.

Corn Ice Cream:
2 cups canned unsweetened coconut milk
1 teaspoon vanilla extract
1/2 cup sugar
Pinch salt
2 cups raw corn kernels
1/4 cup refined coconut oil
1 1/2 cups raw cashews, soaked for at least 6 hours, then drained

Candied Bourbon Pecans:
1/4 cup pecan halves
1/4 cup water
2 tablespoons bourbon
3 tablespoons grated piloncillo or turbinado sugar
1/4 teaspoon salt

In a small pot over medium heat, add the coconut milk, vanilla, sugar, and salt and bring the mixture to a low simmer, reducing to medium-low once it starts bubbling. Once the sugar is melted, add the corn and coconut oil, bring the mixture to a boil, then immediately remove the pot from the heat and let it cool for 1 hour.

Using a strainer, remove 1 cup of corn and set it aside. Purée the remaining corn and liquid in a blender or food processor, then add the reserved corn back to the mix. Transfer to an ice cream maker and follow the ice cream maker's instructions. Alternatively, transfer the ice cream to a freezer-safe bowl and freeze, stirring it with a fork every 20 minutes, so the ice cream doesn't crystallize.

In a small pan, add the pecans, water, bourbon, piloncillo or turbinado sugar, and salt and bring the mixture to a boil over medium-high heat. Once this condenses to syrup, about 5 minutes, remove from the heat and allow the syrup to cool. Coarsely chop the candied pecans. Serve the Corn Ice Cream and sprinkle the Candied Bourbon Pecans on top.

Cocoa-Pistachio Churros
Churros de Cacao y Pistachos

MAKES 4 CHURROS

You can take the basic churro batter and frying technique in this recipe and create your own churro concoctions. I list some of my favorite variations in the sidebar, but this one is sure to impress. Whenever I introduce people to churros, I give them a plain one dressed simply with sugar and cinnamon. It's always a hit. Making these takes a little practice (though you get to eat the "mistakes") in order to get the feel for the dough, the oil, and the size of the churro. You'll need a piping bag and a star tip to make these, so have those handy before you begin.

Churro Batter:

1 cup water

2 tablespoons corn or other vegetable oil, plus more for frying

1 tablespoon plus 1 teaspoon sugar

1/2 teaspoon ground cinnamon

1/3 teaspoon salt

1 cup unbleached all-purpose flour

Cocoa-Pistachio Sugar:

1/2 cup sugar

1/4 cup cocoa powder

1/3 cup finely chopped pistachios

Batter: In a small pot, combine the water, oil, sugar, cinnamon, and salt and bring to a simmer over medium heat. Stir until the sugar dissolves and simmer for 2 to 3 minutes. Remove the pot from the heat and immediately whisk the flour into the pot, whisking vigorously until evenly combined. Allow this to cool.

Cocoa-Pistachio Sugar: Combine the sugar, cocoa powder, and pistachios on a plate so you can roll the churros in the mix. Set the plate near the stove and get a rack or plate and paper towel ready to receive the cooked churros.

Frying: Add 1 inch of oil to a wide iron skillet or heavy-bottomed pan. It needs to be big enough to fit the length of the churro you wish to make. The wider the pan, the more churros you can cook at one time. Bring the oil to 375°F. Transfer the churro batter to a piping bag fixed with a 3/8- or 1/2-inch star tip. Pipe a little batter into the oil. If it browns in about 2 minutes, the oil is ready. Pipe 4- to 5-inch churros into the oil, pinching off the end of the churro with your fingers. Be careful that you don't get spattered with oil.

Fry the churros for 2 to 3 minutes, until they are golden brown. Transfer them to a rack or paper towel and give them about 1 minute to cool. It's important not to wait longer than 1 minute; otherwise, the sugar mix will have a hard time sticking to the churros. Roll them in the Cocoa-Pistachio Sugar and set them aside. Repeat this process until you have cooked all the batter.

About Churros

Churros are versatile goodies—you can alter the flavors by changing the spice mix. I always use 1/2 cup sugar and add other ingredients to the mix. The classic one uses sugar and 1 teaspoon ground cinnamon. Here are some other variations you can try: finely chopped peanuts; minced fresh mint; ground coffee and chiles de árbol; cardamom and black pepper; dried mango powder; and smoked salt.

Flan with Apricot Preserves
Flan con Conservas de Albaricoque

MAKES 4 SERVINGS

This flan is based on a recipe from a nunnery in Puebla that I first learned about in a book called *My Sweet Mexico*. I called the nunnery to talk about the recipe and, while theirs was far from vegan, I was able to create a vegan version of this dessert and put my own twist on it by adding in black pepper and almonds to complement the apricot preserves that top the flan, which replace the traditional cajeta caramel in most standard flans.

2 tablespoons melted vegan butter

3/4 cup plus 3 tablespoons grated piloncillo or brown sugar, divided

2 cups plain unsweetened almond milk, divided, plus more as needed

1 vanilla bean, split lengthwise, or 1 teaspoon vanilla extract

1/4 teaspoon almond extract

6 black peppercorns

1/3 cup cornstarch

1/2 cup apricot preserves

1/4 cup toasted slivered almonds

Brush 4 (4-inch) ramekins with the melted butter, then sprinkle 3 tablespoons of the sugar into them. Set them aside.

In a small pot bring 1 1/2 cups of the milk to a simmer over medium heat and add the vanilla bean, almond extract, peppercorns, and the remaining 3/4 cup sugar. Gently simmer the milk mixture for 10 minutes, then remove and discard the peppercorns. Add more milk to bring the liquid in the pot to 1 1/2 cups if necessary, and return it to a simmer. Make a slurry with the cornstarch and the remaining 1/2 cup milk, then slowly pour the slurry into the pot and whisk until it congeals. Transfer the flan to the ramekins. Chill in the refrigerator for 45 minutes.

When you plate the flan, gently flip the ramekins over onto the serving plates and carefully spread 2 tablespoons of the apricot preserves on each. Sprinkle each serving with the toasted slivered almonds.

Sugar Skulls
Calaveras de Az'car

MAKES 4 SMALL OR 1 MEDIUM SUGAR SKULL

Sugar skulls have become icons that speak to Mexican people as symbols of both beauty and death. They are traditionally made with meringue powder, but you can make an easy vegan version using cornstarch. They're given to family members and friends as gifts for El Día de los Muertos, the Day of the Dead, a holiday celebrating those who have passed beyond. They are often placed on small altars called *ofrendas,* along with marigolds, breads, and other favorite foods and drinks of the dead. They also serve simply as wonderful works of art. You'll want a variety of food colorings to get the most out of your sugar skulls and a piping bag with a small tip for precise work. **Note:** You will need sugar skull molds to make this recipe.

Skulls:
2 cups white sugar
1 teaspoon cornstarch
1 teaspoon water

Place the sugar in a medium bowl. In a small bowl, whisk together the cornstarch and water, then add it to the sugar. Mix the sugar by hand until it is the consistency of wet sand. Transfer the sugar to your skull molds. Many molds have a front and back, and you'll want to press them together once they're filled to make one skull. Alternatively, you have make skulls with flat backs, in which case this recipe will make twice as many skulls. Let the skulls dry for 5 hours, then gently remove them from the molds.

Decorating Cream:
3/4 cup vegan shortening
2 cups sifted confectioners' sugar
2 tablespoons water, or as needed
Food coloring, as needed

In a stand mixer, whip the shortening until it is creamy. Add the confectioners' sugar and continue whipping. Add just enough water to ensure that the mix is thick but not dry. Whip the sugar mixture until fluffy, about 2 to 3 minutes. Divide it among the number of bowls as you see fit and add a small amount of food coloring to each bowl. The amount you need will be dependent on how many times you divide the piping cream. (If you divide it into fourths, you need 1/8 teaspoon food coloring for each bowl. If you divide the cream more or less, adjust accordingly.) Transfer the colored cream into a piping bag with a small tip and decorate the sugar skulls.

Resources

Shopping Online

Shopping for ingredients online is easier than it's ever been. The best place to find your ingredients and equipment is at a Mexican-oriented market, but if you need to source either of those online, the following websites are good places to start. None of these companies endorsed me, these are just my recommendations.

MexGrocer.com. This site has equipment like tortilla presses, corn grinders, metal comales, and molcajetes. It also sells ingredients like piloncillo, achiote paste, and dried chiles. It's a gathering of all the major Mexican utensils and ingredients in one place. www.mexgrocer.com

Bob's Red Mill. A good place to find organic masa harina (corn "flour" for tortillas) and organic whole wheat flour. www.bobsredmill.com

Frontera Fiesta. Chef Rick Bayless's salsas are some of my favorite commercial salsas. If you don't want to make your own salsas, these are a great option with a wide range of heat levels and styles. www.fronterafiesta.com

Penzey's. Specializes in spices and is a great source for dried epazote and good-quality chile powders. www.penzeys.com

La Tienda. Focuses on Spanish goods, but their cazuelas are among the best I've used and it's one of the few brands that don't use lead in their glaze. www.latienda.com

My Toque. Another seller of good-quality cazuelas under the brand La Chamba. They also have other clay cooking items, including the elusive clay comal. www.mytoque.com

Lodge Manufacturing. The website of Lodge Logic, a prolific, good-quality brand of cast iron cookware. Cast iron skillets, grill pans, and griddles are excellent for pan-roasting. www.lodgemfg.com

Epicurean. If you purchase a good knife, you need a good cutting board to go along with it. Not only will a good cutting board make your prep time quicker, it will also protect the edge of your knife. My favorite brand is Epicurean. www.epicureancs.com

Chemex®. These are my favorite coffee pots for brewing a smooth, flavorful coffee. Make sure to get the special filters that go with the coffee pot as they are designed to filter out more of the bitter components in coffee than traditional filters do. www.chemexcoffeemaker.com

A Note about Amazon and eBay

Amazon.com has all of the above items listed on their site, although their standard free shipping offer only applies to a select few of them. You can also visit www.ebay.com for some of the equipment. I was able to get my corn grinder relatively inexpensively that way.

Glossary

The following is a glossary of Spanish terms used throughout this book.

Achiote – A small red seed also called annatto.

Achiote paste – A spice mix made primarily from achiote with several fragrant seeds added to the mix.

Aguas frescas – Refreshing sweetened drinks, usually served chilled.

Ajo – The Spanish word for garlic.

Ancho chile – The dried form of the poblano. Ancho means "wide" in Spanish.

Anejo – Aged for a prolonged time. It can refer to aged alcohol, cheese, and other foods.

Árbol, chile(s) de – This means "tree chiles." They are small, hot chiles and can be found fresh or dried.

Bebidas – Drinks.

Blanco – White, though sometimes it is translated as silver.

Cascabel chiles – Bell-shaped dried red chiles so named because they sound like a rattle.

Cazuela – A glazed clay cooking vessel ideal for stewing ingredients and keeping them warm.

Cebolla – Onion.

Cebollita – Small onion.

Cerveza – Beer.

Champiñones – Mushrooms, usually wild mushrooms.

Chipotles – Smoked, dried jalapeños.

Chorizo – A marinated spicy Mexican ground sausage.

Comal(es) – A metal or clay "pan" ideal for sautéing ingredients and cooking tortillas. Metal comals are flat and oblong and more common than clay comals. Clay comals are slightly curved and are excellent for cooking tortillas.

Epazote – An herb with a bright, acidic flavor.

Frijoles – The Spanish word for beans.

Guajillo chile – A long red chile used as the base for quite a few chile sauces.

Güero(s) (chiles) – Hot, medium-size yellow chiles.

Guisado – A dish of stewed or slow-cooked ingredients.

Habanero – A small, fat orange or yellow chile with very high heat.

Hatch chiles – A unique variety of chile grown in the Hatch Valley of New Mexico.

Hongos – A common word for mushrooms.

Jalapeño – A very common, thick medium-length green chile with medium heat.

Limón – Lime.

Maíz – Corn. This spelling reflects the Taíno use of the word, while "maize" is the Spanish. Maíz is typically used when referring to it in a historical sense.

Maguey – Another name for agave.

Masa – The Spanish word for dough. In Mexico, it almost always refers to corn dough.

Masa Harina – Dried and ground corn that has been specially treated so it can be mixed with water to make corn dough.

Mezcal – An alcohol derived from fire-roasted agave cores.

Mineros – Miners.

Molcajete – A rough mortar traditionally made from lava rock, though some are made from other material, like concrete.

Mojo de ajo – Olive oil that has been roasted with a large amount of garlic and citrus juice.

Mole – A thick sauce that develops over low heat for a long period of time.

Molina – A corn grinder.

Nahuatl – The language spoken by the Aztecs. Nahuatl is an umbrella term for quite a number of different dialects.

Napolitos – Cactus pad strips (see "nopales").

Nejayote – The leftover liquid from making nixtamal.

Nixtamal – Corn that has been specially treated in an alkaline solution and partially cooked. This treatment makes the components of the corn more bioavailable and allows the corn to be ground into masa.

Nopales – Whole cactus pads or strips from the prickly pear cactus.

Pasado chiles – Dried long green chiles.

Pepitas – Green, shelled pumpkin seeds.

Pequín chiles – Small, oblong orange chiles that are very hot.

Piloncillo – A cone of hard unrefined sugar.

Plancha – A very large, flat metal cooking surface usually found in restaurants or at large taco stands.

Poblano chile – A large green chile frequently roasted for sauces or for turning into strips called "rajas."

Pozole – Corn that has been nixtamalized and fully cooked.

Queso – Cheese.

Queso fresco – Fresh cheese.

Rajas – Strips of roasted green chiles.

Rojo – Red.

Serrano chile – A medium-length thin green chile that is hot but not unbearably hot.

Soya de Carne – Spanish for TVP or "soy meat."

Sudados – A Spanish word that means "sweated." Tacos de Canasta are sometimes called Tacos Sudados.

Tejolote – The pestle for the molcajete, used to bash and grind ingredients.

Teosinte – A type of grass and the genetic predecessor to corn.

Tequila – Alcohol distilled from agave syrup. The syrup is typically extracted from the agave plant by steaming or pressure cooking it.

Tortilladora – A tortilla press.

Tortillero – A tortilla warmer. Also the name for someone who makes tortillas.

Vegano – The Spanish word for "vegan."

Verde – Green.

Verduras – The Spanish word for "vegetables."

Acknowledgments

My thanks go out to my wife, Madelyn, for her support and encouragement; my publisher Jon Robertson of Vegan Heritage Press for his support and encouragement, as well; to my team of recipe testers for providing valuable time and feedback; to my family for their willingness to share our family recipes and stories; and to the cooks out there who are crafting delicious, compassionate Mexican cuisine. Keep up the good work!

About the Author

Chef Jason Wyrick is the author of *Vegan Tacos* and food editor of *Living the Farm Sanctuary Life.* He is also the executive chef of The Vegan Taste. In 2001, Jason was diagnosed with diabetes in his midtwenties and was told he would have to be on medication for the rest of his life. Instead, Jason chose to become

vegan, reversed his diabetes in eight months, and lost over 100 pounds over the course of two years. Along the way, he learned about factory farming, and that cemented his decision to become vegan. He also learned that food had to be outstanding, or no one was going to eat it. He then left his job as the director of marketing for a computer company in order to become a chef and help others learn how to eat healthfully, compassionately, and well.

Since then, he has coauthored the *New York Times* Bestselling book *21 Day Weight Loss Kickstart* with Neal Barnard, MD, and has taught alongside Dr. Barnard, Dr. John McDougall, and Dr. Gabriel Cousens. Jason became the first vegan culinary instructor in the world-famous Le Cordon Bleu program through the Scottsdale Culinary Institute, founded the world's first vegan food magazine, *The Vegan Culinary Experience,* has presented for the American Dietetic Association and the American Diabetes Association, Humana, The Wellness Community, Farm Sanctuary, and is a regular guest at the Scottsdale Culinary Festival.

He has catered for prestigious organizations, including Google, the Frank Lloyd Wright Foundation, PETA, and Farm Sanctuary and has been featured in the *New York Times,* and on both local and national television. He has taught hundreds of vegan cooking classes across the United States and has taught internationally in both Costa Rica and Italy. His recipes have appeared in *Vegetarian Times* and have been featured in several of Dr. Barnard's books. Most of all, Chef Jason loves good food and sharing it with others.

Metric Conversions and Equivalents

The recipes in this book have not been tested with metric measurements, so some variations may occur.

LIQUID	
US	**METRIC**
1 tsp	5 ml
1 tbs	15 ml
2 tbs	30 ml
1/4 cup	60 ml
1/3 cup	75 ml
1/2 cup	120 ml
2/3 cup	150 ml
3/4 cup	180 ml
1 cup	240 ml
1 1/4 cups	300 ml
1 1/3 cups	325 ml
1 1/2 cups	350 ml
1 2/3 cups	375 ml
1 3/4 cups	400 ml
2 cups (1 pint)	475 ml
3 cups	720 ml
4 cups (1 quart)	945 ml

LENGTH	
US	**Metric**
1/2 inch	1.25 cm
1 inch	2.5 cm
6 inches	15 cm
8 inches	20 cm
10 inches	25 cm
12 inches	30 cm

GENERAL METRIC CONVERSION FORMULAS	
Ounces to grams	ounces x 28.35 = grams
Grams to ounces	grams x 0.035 = ounces
Pounds to grams	pounds x 435.5 = grams
Pounds to kilograms	pounds x 0.45 = kilograms
Cups to liters	cups x 0.24 = liters
Fahrenheit to Celsius	(°F - 32) x 5 ÷ 9 = °C
Celsius to Fahrenheit	(°C x 9) ÷ 5 + 32 = °F

WEIGHT	
US	**METRIC**
1/2 oz	14 g
1 oz	28 g
1 1/2 oz	43 g
2 oz	57 g
2 1/2 oz	71 g
4 oz	113 g
5 oz	142 g
6 oz	170 g
7 oz	200 g
8 oz (1/2 lb)	227 g
9 oz	255 g
10 oz	284 g
11 oz	312 g
12 oz	340 g
13 oz	368 g
14 oz	400 g
15 oz	425 g
16 oz (1 lb)	454 g

OVEN TEMPERATURE		
°F	**Gas Mark**	**°C**
250	1/2	120
275	1	140
300	2	150
325	3	165
350	4	180
375	5	190
400	6	200
425	7	220
450	8	230
475	9	240
500	10	260
550	Broil	290

Index